grieving

grieving

a beginner's guide

jerusha hull mccormack

The heart of the wise is in the house of mourning;
but the heart of fools is in the house of mirth.

Ecclesiastes 7:4

DARTON·LONGMAN + TODD

For David and Thomas
and all those who have
come down this road with me –
particularly JGB.

First published in 2005 by
Darton, Longman and Todd Ltd
1 Spencer Court
140–142 Wandsworth High Street
London SW18 4JJ

ISBN 0–232–52629–X

A catalogue record for this book is available from the British Library.

Designed and produced by Sandie Boccacci
Phototypeset in 10.25/12.5pt Palatino
Printed and bound in Great Britain by
CPI, Bath

contents

where we begin

Chances are, if you are reading this, your heart is broken. There are many things that can break a heart: the death of someone loved; the loss of a marriage; the end of a career; emigration or exile or even moving house. For those who have the capacity to love, whether it is a person or a pet or a place, their loss can be devastating.

This short book is designed to help those in pain – and specifically those who have lost someone through death – to imagine the path before them. It is a path of suffering. But it is also a path that may lead to unexpected discoveries – and to peace. There is no sure route; or rather, there are many routes. The purpose of this book is to provide the reader with a series of signposts by which they may find their own path to a new life.

I do not speak as a therapist or a counsellor, simply as someone who has once lost someone and whose whole life changed after that. I make no apology for this. We are all amateurs at grief; it comes to us all; we must all go through it. Some of us make extraordinary discoveries while doing so. To treat grief as a problem to be fixed, or (worse still) to medicalize it, is to rob us of the extraordinary privilege of encountering this experience on our terms: for each of us has our own way of grieving, and each of us has something special to learn from the process. In my own case, when my husband died, none of our friends had gone through a similar ordeal. They tried to help, and they did; but I was isolated from any community of like experience. What I found more difficult was that, after the first year, there was little public recognition or even patience for my grieving, although I realized that the pain I was in was one of the most intense experiences of my life. I knew instinctively it was also one of the most important, that how I handled that suffering would either make or break me; it would determine the quality of the rest of my life. And yet it seemed that all everyone else wanted me to do was to 'recover' as soon as possible.

This confusion was compounded by the fact that, once the funeral was over, existing conventions dictated no clear path for me to follow. A century ago, I would have been wearing black for a year, ensuring that my loss would have been publicly acknowledged and thus honoured. I would have been allowed to withdraw from formal commitments for a decent length of time. It would even have been acknowledged that I might never 'recover'; for instance, in Victorian times widows did not often remarry. But in this day and age, I was expected to return to full-time work within months. Within a year, people were asking whether I had 'recovered' yet – and whether I was dating.

Yet inside, I was lost. I had little idea of what to expect, and was shocked by the way others casually compounded my loss. Of course I lost income; but I also lost status; suddenly it seemed I had become a very marginal person. Some friends were exceptional; and others who had not previously been close stepped in to help in unexpected ways. But it was hard to disguise the fact that, over time, the phone calls and invitations dwindled away and that, in the end, I could count on only a faithful few to call or invite me out on any reliable basis. It was as if society wanted to forget – not so much *me*, as the kind of pain I represented.

And yet, although lost, and in pain, I knew somehow I would find a way to heal. In fact, I discovered not one way, but many. But finding those ways was like struggling through unknown territory, much like those areas of old maps that used to be marked 'terra incognita'. Ridiculous, I thought, when everyone must travel through this place not once, but several times during a lifetime. So I tried to note the routes I took, and to assemble them into a series of models or maps to help those in grief to imagine the path ahead of them.

For by the very act of imaging that path, the pain itself is transformed. You begin to acknowledge its value and importance. You learn how to stay with the pain, and even to attend to it, so that, in the end, you can make it your own. And, in the process, grieving becomes something else, a resource that has become a reservoir, a support for others, a wound that initiates us into a new chance for life.

What I came to in the end was that grieving, expressed openly and honestly, can be one of the most liberating experiences of life. And yet I found the discourse used for grieving to be quite degraded, in common with the public perception of the experience itself; it seemed that even the most articulate people could be reduced to dog-eared truisms. One made allowances, reminding oneself that they did not know what to say. Or that the available words are often only those that implicitly devalue the fierce power of grief.

Yet, as a consequence, those in mourning would sometimes find themselves trapped in a conspiracy of clichés, all of which tend to represent their state as being something less than it is. 'Bereavement' means a robbery – a loss; how can the grieving counter by saying what they have gained? To be a 'widow' means, by origin, to be emptied; how can the widow explain that she has become something more, not something less, for her encounter with sorrow?

For, liberated from the old, shop-worn clichés, grieving may become another kind of occurrence altogether: a voyage out to the limits of one's known world. Death lies at the frontier of our experience, and to face it openly and honestly may lead us to surprising conclusions.

In charting the way I took, I am conscious that at times it was new only to me – that many others had been there before. I have read their doleful accounts and taken note of sound advice where I could find it. But none tackled the question of how to live through this experience so that its value would not be diminished. And certainly no one else seemed to think of grieving in terms of a quest – or even considered that, properly attended to, discoveries could be made during this process which could transform one's life hereafter.

Accordingly, I have tried to provide another sort of manual for the bereaved. It is less a consolatory piece than a tour guide, which comes complete with the kind of practical advice you will need on your journey, as well as a series of directions which seek to lead you away from the dead-ends of conventional grieving towards new and unexpected horizons. In the end, one can only point to these, for they depend on the traveller having the courage to leave the most well-worn paths in the first place.

This is only a guide, and acknowledges, ultimately, that the road you find will be your own. Each of us grieves in our own way. But if we can do so with a mind open to the unexpected, who knows what resources we will uncover, or what new territory lies beyond the dreary reaches of our pain? We owe it to ourselves to try to find out and, in doing so, to explore the limits of this experience, to see if we can find there a new life – one which is larger, more various, and more surprising than the one that, even now, disappears in our wake.

one: the resources of pain

Life is pain.
(Sophocles)

If this is the first encounter you have had with death, you have entered one of the most intense periods of your life. It may also become the most important, in the sense that it will define the person you will become for the rest of your life.

In encountering death, you are now at the very centre of human experience. You are in the presence of the sacred. Do not let anyone minimize its importance or make you feel that grieving is anything other than an absorbing, life-changing experience.

Others may not necessarily understand this. To them, you are simply someone in 'grief'. They will talk of grief solemnly, as if it were a single thing, which it is not. Grief is an overwhelming experience. It is like acute pain, in the way it can swallow up your entire consciousness. Like acute pain, it can involve a period of shock, or numbness. But when that wears off, one may feel anything, from relief, to anger, to fear.

Grief is not one emotion and no one emotion is appropriate for the grieving. People react to loss in different ways at different times and in different situations. But usually the first reaction to grief is that it is like pain. This can be a useful analogy in several ways.

As in physical pain, you feel wounded. The shock of the pain can numb you. You may be able to think of nothing else except the pain.

A certain numbness is an entirely natural reaction. It is nature's way of protecting you from the pain you are in.

During this first phase, it may be helpful to imagine yourself as bruised and broken, like the victim of a bad car accident (and maybe that is precisely what you are).

What follows from this?

for those in pain

From the very first moment, you must take good care of yourself physically. You will never be able to endure the pain you are in, unless you take what measures you can to sustain your physical self.

If, in eating, you can't keep much down, eat what you can. Take vitamin supplements.

If you can't sleep, remember this is common in grieving. Doze, take naps. Trust your body to rest when it must.

Remember, this is only pain. It is natural; it is almost normal. Open yourself to the pain. It will not kill you. In fact, it is a sign you are alive.

But you must protect yourself.

Go on a newsfast. Do not watch television, do not read the papers. You are at the moment very raw, very vulnerable. You do not know what you will see when you turn on the news; sudden images of pain may feel like an assault. Remember, television is a very 'hot' medium and invites an immediate emotional reaction. But even printed images can give you pain. Why seek it out? You have enough of your pain to cope with right now; avoid, if possible, picking up on impersonal pain, such as the news.

In the same spirit, see only the people you like and trust. Avoid others if at all possible. If not, minimize contact.

Abandon yourselves to your friends. Ask those close to you to make the necessary arrangements for the funeral and other gatherings. Consult with them, but do not try to take the entire burden of managing practical things at this moment upon yourself. Remember others are grieving too, and helping you in practical matters will also help them to express their own feelings.

Try to free up as much time as possible to allow you to begin to come to terms with what has happened to you. Grieving slows you down in any case; you must insist that others give you space to heal.

Do things in your own time. Do not be rushed into decisions. Do things as you can. If possible, postpone the funeral for a few days until you have had time to decide what to do there.

Do not feel, after the funeral, that you have to clear out things precipitately. Clear things out when you are ready and as you wish to clear them.

Try to avoid anaesthetics: if you drink alcohol, be moderate; avoid sleeping tablets unless absolutely necessary.

Try to notice what helps you get through the day, however small or insignificant. Make a list of such things, and try to do them every day. (For a time, I found 'taking showers' at the top of my list.)

Trust that the pain will be bearable. Even when it does not seem so, the body has its own innate sanity. Ultimately you will sleep when you have to, or at least you will be able to doze. Ultimately, you will be able to eat something. Trust that your body, as well as your mind, has an inborn balance which will begin to assert itself if you allow it to do so.

nothing is right

With grieving comes the sense that nothing is right. The sense of order and predictability in our world is shattered. Often this sense that nothing is right takes the form of bodily disruption. You may not eat or sleep properly. You may have nightmares. You may feel you cannot even get physically comfortable.

You may find you cannot concentrate. You may become absurdly forgetful. This is all normal. You are entirely pre-occupied now; your whole mind and soul is trying to come to terms with that which is unimaginable, unthinkable, and almost impossible to articulate: the ultimate fact of death.

Things may seem chaotic; you may find it hard to organize things or just do them mechanically. Ask others to help whenever possible.

Death can bring enormous practical disruptions. It is not surprising that you may feel disoriented by the sudden change, or feel that everything seems chaotic. Try to bear with the situation and handle it as it comes. In the longer term, things will fall again into place.

Families in grief can also become very dysfunctional. Rather than drawing you closer together, the grief may seem to be driving you apart. Two parents grieving for a child may find themselves locked in mutual silence. If a parent has died, there may be ugly quarrels about the funeral arrangements or about the legal division of a house or other inherited things. Old sibling rivalries may be revived, or family members may seem to be competing for possession of the lost one's presence by claiming that he or she was closest to the dead person, or trying to possess the dead person by appropriating his/her things, or personal papers, or even the control of his/her memory.

Be aware of these pitfalls and try to detach yourself for the time being. In the first onslaught of grief, you need to protect yourself. Remember that at its most intense, grief will challenge every resource within a person, and some react to this challenge by acting out, others by denying their fear or hurt. So try to stand back. Remember that nothing is right for you; but nothing is right for them either, nor for any of the group of which they are a part.

It will take time, and a certain compassion to bring things around. But in the early days, despite your need for comfort, it is best to expect that things will not go smoothly, that others will not necessarily act well all the time, and that arrangements can go awry. It is not a disaster – simply a reflection of the immense disruption that death brings. Be grateful for what goes well, but be prepared for a certain level of emotional and practical chaos.

the importance of pain

You may feel little during the first days or weeks. This is normal. It is nature's way of protecting you from overwhelming pain.

When you begin to register the pain, it is a sign you are beginning to heal. Fortunately, the pain of a great loss often lets itself into consciousness very gradually. This allows you to absorb it little by little. It is a blessing.

It is important to stay open to the pain. Try to detach yourself sufficiently to attend to it on its own terms; not as inherently good or bad, but simply as itself. This pain is yours. It has things to teach you. And, most importantly, it is a sign you are still alive.

You are wounded, and you are hurting. But remember: the instincts of your mind and body are all toward healing.

I like a look of Agony,
Because I know it's true –
Men do not sham Convulsion,
Nor simulate, a Throe –

The eyes glaze once – and that is Death –
Impossible to feign
The Beads opon the Forehead
By homely Anguish strung.

Emily Dickinson

dead-end: pain as damage/mutilation

In modern society, we learn that pain is bad. We actively seek to avoid or deaden pain – or even discomfort or inconvenience. When pain is inevitable, we then have few resources to deal with it. We tend to want to treat it quickly, so that it will go away. You will be offered drugs – everything from sedatives to sleeping tablets. Consider their use carefully.

While it is reasonable to use the new technology of drugs to help us through physical pain, it is dangerous to use them over long periods to dull psychic pain. Also, there are times when the pain simply will not be dulled.

The psyche has its own ways of dealing with pain. The numbness of the first days or weeks is itself a way that it uses to protect itself.

When that numbness wears off, it is important to try to get away from the notion that pain = bad. You may feel damaged. You may feel mutilated. But you are still yourself. You do have the capacity to become whole again. Remember that the entire instinct of your being is to try to heal – and that pain itself is part of that process.

One technique for coping is to shift the way you think about pain. Even while you protect yourself in practical ways (see above), it is important to try to imagine how the pain may be experienced not as negative but as positive.

reorientation: grieving as hurt, hurt as healing

Imagine yourself as physically wounded. What do you do? If you are wounded, you do not cover it up and pretend it doesn't exist. If you are wounded, you open up the wound to clean it, so it will heal.

tell everyone:

Honour the wound. If you try to ignore it, it will grow infected. If it were a literal wound, ignoring it could even kill you. But this is a wound to your spirit. Others cannot see it. So it is even more important not to hide it, but to let others know you are in pain.

Remember, unlike a physical wound, it will not register with those you meet, so it may be necessary to inform or remind them of your situation. Do this as early in a conversation as possible to prevent yourself being trapped by others' assumptions. Remember that in a society where there are no longer any tokens by which the grieving may be easily identified – such as the old custom of wearing black – it is necessary for you to give the sign early to avoid compounding your own hurt.

keep in mind: what has happened to you is important

Do not deny the wound. Do not deny the pain. And do not allow others to disregard or minimize your pain. (By doing so, they may think they are helping you, but in fact the opposite is true.)

find a sacred space

A sacred space is one in which you can heal. It should be one which is quiet and offers comfort: a bench in a favourite park; a place where you once walked with the one you loved; a spot near the grave; a forest clearing. It does not matter where it is as long as it is quiet and responds to your condition. As for myself, I went back to the church of my childhood. It was not only that the ritual was consoling but that, within the community of the church, I found a place where suffering was taken seriously. There I could acknowledge my pain and begin to become whole again.

imagine yourself as healing

A tree wounded in its trunk by a hard object simply grows around it. You too are growing, and as you grow, you will surround the hard thing that has wounded you. It will not kill you. Although you have been hurt, you can still grow and flourish.

Likewise when you heal, you will have a scar. It will always remind you – and others – of the wound you have suffered. In time, it will simply become part of you, and at times, it will even hurt again, in a way that reminds you distantly of the intense pain immediately after the event.

This scar is a good thing. It is the memento of the suffering we have endured. It is a sign that we continue to endure, but have never forgotten the wound and the loss by which it was made.

when pain is good:
When it tells you you have to pay attention to it.
When it breaks you open, making you bigger.
When it connects you with the pain of others.
When it forces you to look at the world differently.
When it reminds you that you are alive.
When it compels you to be honest.
When it makes you understand that it is inevitable.
When you recognize it as one of the most intense, and potentially
    valuable, experiences in your life.

The images we have in our head for pain are almost always negative. For this reason, it is important to try to find new images, or models, for pain that imply something positive. The following are two that are most helpful in understanding the ways that pain can be thought of as good:

reorientation: pain as an initiation rite
In traditional societies, almost all initiation rites involve pain. The way the pain is endured is often important to the value of the rite; but of most importance, for our purposes, is that pain itself is recognized as a gateway experience, one that leads us into a new life. In our own case, this initiation is not (as rites the anthropologists describe) into the company of warriors, or of sexually mature men and women – but into the vast and invisible brotherhood of pain, by which we become at last fully human.

Such thinking is very ancient. The Greek god Dionysus was said to be born out of a wound in Zeus's thigh. When he was an infant, he was torn apart by the jealous Titans. But they overlooked his heart, from which a new body was reconstituted.

Dionysus is the icon of the wounded god; born of a wound

that became a womb, and reborn again after being fatally dismembered. Thus he becomes the prototype of how, in life, we can be made whole after we have been rent.

For Christians the prototype is that of the Christ broken upon the cross. Because this image is one of terrible pain, it speaks to those also in pain. But I prefer the Christ to whom St Bernard prays:

> Conceal me, Wound; within thy cave
> Locked fast, no thing shall harm me;
> There let me nestle close and safe,
> There soothe my soul and warm me.

For this is a motherly Christ, who makes of his mortal wound a space within which the soul may be safe to grow again, until it, like the Christ himself, is born into a new life.

Although ancient, these images of pain as initiation endure. Thus, in a modern story involving fatal illness, one observer meditates on the effect to the sufferer, and how, 'through the little hole of his wound, the immense realm of the spirit enters'.

Our loss is more than a little hole. But the space it opens may become like a door opening into another world.

We may discover that door only slowly, groping through the darkness of our grieving. It is there, and when it swings open, another world also opens to us.

Thus the rite of initiation can provide a kind of map for what lies ahead. Keeping that model in mind may help us to bear our pain and to be patient with it, allowing it to take its course.

It may also give us hope that this wound, too, may become a space which will open to us the immense realm of the spirit.

reorientation: the pain of childbirth

In terms of comparable experience, the early days after bereavement seemed to replay, for me, the shock, the chaos, the terrible uncertainty of a first childbirth.

As in a first childbirth, you do not know exactly what to expect. Like childbirth, death brings chaos, emotional as well as actual. You will not know how you will feel from one moment to the next. Everything feels like an emergency, yet, amidst the chaos, much must be planned. Admit the chaos; go with it. Try not to panic; organize what you can and leave the rest to others. As in childbirth, you now know you are dependent on others to help you through.

As in childbirth, also, you must expect real pain. Remember that this pain is not a sign you are going to die, even if you feel as if you might. Trust yourself to bear it. In fact, the exercises associated with natural childbirth (a modified version of yoga breathing and meditation exercises) can be very useful during the early days of grieving.

What these exercises try to teach you is that, while you will be in pain, the pain itself can be greatly exacerbated by fear. Therefore, to exorcise the fear, you must accept the pain, breathing your way through the worst of it. If you can trust yourself to bear it, the pain can in fact become bearable. The great enemy is fear – of the unknown, of the pain itself. Fear will make you tighten up; it can actually incapacitate you. It is natural to fear pain; but pain in childbirth is the price of a new life.

Not all of us go through childbirth. But if you can imagine it, the model of giving birth is an empowering one for many reasons. First of all, it is a model which acknowledges that pain is inevitable. Secondly, it is a model which presents the pain as bearable. Finally, childbirth as a model implies what is actually the case: that pain can be a productive force, from which you will be able to create a new life out of yourself.

At first it may not seem so. But slowly, over months and years, you will find another life growing within you, and seeking to be born.

The work of grieving moves towards acceptance of grieving, which entails an acceptance of pain.

Pay attention to the pain; it is not all negative. It has things to teach you.

LIV

Oh yet we trust that somehow good
    Will be the final goal of ill,
    To pangs of nature, sins of will,
Defects of doubt, and taints of blood;

That nothing walks with aimless feet;
    That not one life shall be destroyed,
    Or cast as rubbish to the void,
When God hath made the pile complete;

That not a worm is cloven in vain;
    That not a moth with vain desire
    Is shriveled in a fruitless fire,
Or but subserves another's gain.

Behold, we know not anything;
    I can but trust that good shall fall
    At last – far off – at last, to all,
And every winter change to spring.

So runs my dream: but what am I?
    An infant crying in the night:
    An infant crying for the light:
With no more language but a cry.

Alfred, Lord Tennyson,
'In Memoriam A.H.H.'

two: imagine

Death defies the human imagination. We cannot imagine what it is like to die. And yet, we must imagine it, since dying is an inevitable part of our lives.

In the seventeenth century, dying was considered an art and was even practised as such. This is because among believing Christians, a good death was taken as a sign that one would be saved, in religious terms. In Buddhist thinking, the state of one's mind at death determines how one will be reincarnated. So one seeks to die well.

In our present time, we do not seek good deaths. The very term is regarded as an offensive contradiction. For death is considered a bad thing in modern society – a sign of failure, a signing off from our collective obsession with keeping things as they are – or simply with keeping things, full stop. It reminds us that people, unlike things, do not keep and are not meant to be kept.

So, to contain death, we minimize or deny it. We avoid thinking about, never mind imagining, our own deaths.

What a bereavement does is open us up to death. Our own death now has a new immediacy. What do we do with this new experience? Most people want to shut it down, and most people around us would like us to shut it down: they want us to 're-cover' the kind of equanimity we had before all this happened and return to our former, relatively insensate selves.

But if we are to come to understand what grieving does for us, we cannot ever return to that state. Our work now is to keep our life open towards death. In so doing, we come to understand the true meaning of love as well as that of pain and sorrow within the context of that interdependent, shifting organism we call creation. That act of understanding is what we call imagination.

To choose not to keep oneself open towards death is to

choose a half-life, a dreary existence from which all that is mysterious and inexplicable is excluded. Our present life in the relatively wealthy countries of the West preaches a pursuit of happiness and the making of money. In this life, fear and mystery are banished by the distractions of work and pleasure; suffering is regarded as merely an unfortunate accident. Our culture refuses to accept that pain can bring us insight, and may allow us to see, with the inner eye, the true source of our humanity: that through suffering we are able to discover the very fountain of life, and of joy; for without pain, there can be no joy.

dead-end: denying the death

Yet, even if we think we may be prepared, often the first response to the news of a death is a visceral one: you may find yourself with every fibre of your being shouting silently inside, 'No! No! No! This can't be happening.'

What people say on this occasion will seem to be only words, and the words they use – such as 'dead' – may mean little or nothing to you. Your brain will simply refuse to accept the information as given.

If something like this happens to you, do not think it strange. In modern society, we seldom witness a death at close hand. It is regarded as unusual, rather than inevitable, that people die. And when they die, they are often either very sick or very old, so somehow the death seems more 'natural', more acceptable – or, at the very least, we have had some warning.

But even then, deep inside, we never accept death easily. It is not only society or the way we die, it's just that we cannot imagine not being here ourselves, so it is very hard to accept it if someone else disappears. This is the way humans are wired, it seems. And in some ways it is a blessing, because it means that the reality of death dawns on us very slowly; our mind will not take in more of actuality than it can handle, and in the very first shock of a death, what it can handle may be very little indeed.

The same goes for our grieving. The losses which accompany death may seem in time to multiply, but we take them in only gradually. Then we start to feel very alone, as if the person we loved were the only person who had ever died. But if we insist that we alone are the only ones to suffer, we isolate ourselves from the very source of our consolation: that, although our sorrow is great and is in some sense uniquely ours, death eventually touches all of us. That recognition helps bind us together and will allow us, eventually, to be released from our grieving.

This paradox is recognized in the story of Kisa Gotami from *The Tibetan Book of the Dead*:

> Kisa Gotami's first baby fell ill and died before it was a year old. Grief-stricken and unable to accept that death, she carried the dead child from house to house asking for help to find someone to cure him.
>
> Everywhere she was laughed at and ridiculed. Eventually someone directed her to the Great Healer. He listened to her petition and agreed to help her. 'The only thing that will heal your child,' he said, 'is a pinch of mustard seed from the house of a family where no one has ever died.'
>
> Kisa Gotami gladly went away to begin her search. She went from house to house, from village to village, but nowhere could she find a family where none had died.
>
> When she went back to the Great Healer, he told her gently, 'Did you imagine that you alone had lost someone you greatly loved? All living things are subject to one unchanging law – the Prince of Death, who like a raging torrent bears all things towards the sea.'
>
> 'Teach me the truth,' Kisa Gotami said. 'Teach me what is beyond death, and what there is within me that will not die.'
>
> 'There is only one way out of the ocean of unbearable suffering, of the endless cycle of birth and death,' answered the Buddha. 'Pain has made you learn, and to follow the path to liberation through enlightenment ...'

dead-end: avoiding the pain

People may tell you:

Don't try to see the body; it will upset you. Don't bother going in to say goodbye; after all, he/she is dead.

Don't bring the children; or (worse):

Don't tell the children what has happened.

Or even: Don't bother going to the funeral; after all, it is quite inconvenient and you are doing work here that is important and shouldn't be interrupted. (This rings particularly true if you are abroad, say, and getting back would mean considerable expense or practical difficulty.)

These people are only trying to save you from pain. But you cannot avoid the pain, and the pain is, in fact, more bearable if you are able to confront it directly. Go see the body, if you can, and try to say goodbye.

If the person who died is important to you, go to the funeral and join with others in their grieving.

Avoiding seeing the body, or deciding not to attend a funeral is something people do all the time. It is a mistake, although it may be months or years before this is clear.

Even more common is an avoidance of words associated with death. Faced with the difficult task of telling others that someone has died, people often resort to euphemisms.

But it is important, in confronting death, to use the most direct words available. Euphemisms will not soften the blow; they only deflect it, so that you cannot begin to register openly what is actually happening.

Thus, when you have to tell others the news about what has happened, use the word 'dead'. Say 'He is dead' or 'She died an hour ago'. Do not be tempted to use other phrases, such as the following:

'He passed away.'
'She is no longer with us.'
'He has gone.'
'We've lost her.'
'She has gone to her reward/to heaven.'
'He is with the angels.'

'He is at rest.'

'She is asleep at last.' (Particularly with children, this leads to enormous confusion.)

All such phrases prevent you from encountering this experience openly and honestly. And if you are ever to come to terms with what has happened to you, it is important to encounter this event with as few defences as possible. It is going to be hard enough to accept that someone you love is dead; using imprecise, sentimental, or euphemistic language delays that acceptance and prevents you from making the first steps towards healing.

reorientation: full-frontal encounter

Imagination begins in experience. Unless you allow yourself to encounter this loss in as direct a way as possible, you will lose the experience on which you must build.

say goodbye in person

Therefore: if at all possible, go in to see the body of the person you have lost. Seek some private time in its presence. Talk to the person you loved. Patch up any outstanding quarrels. Tell them how you feel. Tell them what you hope to do now. Ask forgiveness for any unfinished business. Then say goodbye.

This is an important step. It may be difficult, and it may be a shock, but it is also very comforting. Often people report that they felt the person they loved was listening and understood what was being said. They found that saying goodbye in person proved to be a grounding experience. It places you face to face with the most important fact right now: the person you love is dead. That alone will help you to evade your own powers of denial.

construct a narrative

The next thing you will need about this death is a story. You need to surround this event with a narrative, precisely because, in the end, you will never understand it – because death defies

I heard a Fly buzz – when I died –
The Stillness in the Room
Was like the Stillness in the Air –
Between the Heaves of Storm –

The Eyes around – had wrung them dry –
And Breaths were gathering firm
For that last Onset – when the King
Be witnessed – in the Room –

I willed my Keepsakes – Signed away
What portion of me be
Assignable – and then it was
There interposed a Fly –

With Blue – uncertain – stumbling Buzz –
Between the light – and me –
And then the Windows failed – and then
I could not see to see –

Emily Dickinson

our human logic. Yet it is necessary, as human beings, to try to understand it.

Thus any – and every – reliable narrative will help. If you were not there when the death occurred, try to find out as much information about what happened as possible. Draw on every source: witnesses, police, doctors, autopsies. (Normally, all sudden or unexplained deaths require an autopsy by law. Do note that if you are a close relative, not only do you have the right to an autopsy report, but also the right to go over it with the doctor in charge at the time of the death. This is an invaluable chance to ask questions about a sudden death and to get answers that may be helpful in understanding how this came about.)

Only when you have all this information will you be able to embark on the important work of imagining how your loss came about. And, however difficult and even horrendous the details may be, it is better to know the facts now than to be prey to questions later, when the facts perhaps can no longer be recovered.

stay open; stay honest

When you have this information, it is important to be open about it. If you wish to conceal aspects of it, that is OK, as long as you are prepared to be honest in what you do not conceal. It is crucial that children be told what has happened, in terms that they can understand.

If there is an aspect of the event about which there might be public shame (the person was drunk, or on drugs, or committed suicide), honesty and openness are even more important. Death is one of those events which strip away falsity. If you are to heal, it is important to deal with the facts, not fantasies or half-truths. Silence or evasion is preferable, if you cannot bring yourself to share the truth immediately with those around you. But you can be sure it will be known eventually, so it is better to be open about it now. More importantly: being open with others is the only way you can possibly come to terms with the facts yourself.

avoid secrets

The difficulty with constructing a narrative is that, inevitably, it will give a false sense of order or even a rationale to an event that is profoundly irrational. Nevertheless, the facts are comforting and do help us to accept that this is what happened and how it happened.

But, then, there are the secrets. Sometimes these are the secrets of the deceased. There are stories of letters found in drawers, or of photographs discovered of a person unknown, but clearly close to the deceased. Even more dramatically, there are stories of an appearance after the funeral of a previously unknown lover or child.

These are the secrets that are disclosed. They may add to the pain or, given a certain generosity of mind, might even help to ease it. It depends on whether you are ready to acknowledge that the person you loved also loved others, and whether you are able to accept these others in the name of that love.

These are not the worst secrets or the ones that necessarily do damage. The worst secrets are the ones you, for some reason or other, have promised to keep: the secret of the survivor who does not disclose that a parent or sibling was a suicide; the secret of the child who tries to cover up his parent's indiscretions or debts from those who have a crucial claim on this information.

The problem with such secrets is that they take on a life of their own. They twist and torment those who must keep them. If you keep such a secret in the dark, that is where it will grow and find its power. This is what the movie star Charlotte Rampling said in retrospect about the confidence she was asked to keep about her sister's suicide in order to protect her mother:

> If I were to advise anyone, I'd say you mustn't run away. You must face it. Because you can't alleviate your own suffering and you can't alleviate suffering for other people. You can't take away someone else's right to suffer as much as you are [suffering]. So my father, you see, had no right actually not to allow my mother to cope with the truth.

The real problem with secrets is that they make you powerless. The actual secret is just a fact. One person's secret is another person's commonplace. A suicide [for instance] is a reality. And reality is reality. But if reality is not let in, if it's kept in the dark, then that is where the secret draws its strength. It draws all strength to itself and to the keeping of the secret.

One can extend this observation to many other facts to which, after a death, others are routinely sworn to silence, even though suicide and extra-marital affairs and bad debts and unacknowledged children are actually more frequent than might be supposed. If you learn of such a fact – and are urged to keep it quiet – perhaps you should regard this circumstance simply as something that has happened.

For, kept in the dark, such facts may become monsters. Only when the light of day is allowed to shine on them do we see them for what they are: events for which we bear no responsibility, except that of acknowledging them. Finally, by taking these facts on board, you will allow the dead person to remain part of your life – not as you wished them to be, perhaps, but as they were and as they are. Acceptance will make you free.

expect the unexpected

One friend once said to me: 'Amazing things happened as my wife was dying. I look at them now and I realize they were miracles. But somehow, in retelling them, they seem to have become a bit shabby – almost as if I had made them up, or they were the result of wishful thinking. But I know they happened, and they made it easier for me to accept that she was dying.'

When you are encountering death, you are on the frontier of human experience. Ordinary measures of what we understand or how we live or how we feel do not always apply. The important thing is to acknowledge that unusual things do happen. Accept these events on their own terms.

And remind yourself that you are now in an unprecedented situation. It is important to trust yourself enough to observe what you feel without judgement. Do not tell others if you feel in some way that they will somehow belittle the significance of

Methought I saw my late espoused saint
Brought to me like Alcestis from the
grave,
Whom Jove's great son to her glad
husband gave,
Rescued from death by force though
pale and faint.
Mine as whom washed from spot of
childbed taint,
Purification in the old Law did save,
And such, as yet once more I trust to
have
Full sight of her in heaven without
restraint,
Came vested all in white, pure as her mind:
Her face was veiled, yet to my fancied
sight,
Love, sweetness, goodness in her
person shined
So clear, as in no face with more delight.
But O as to embrace me she inclined
I waked, she fled, and day brought
back my night.

John Milton, 'Sonnet XIX'

what you are experiencing. This is your journey of exploration. You may discover new things about yourself and your world that will help act as guides to your future. But most of all, take possession of your experience and trust it, however fierce, however inappropriate or even bizarre at times it may seem.

the circles of purgatory

One night while out on a walk, I met a friend whose adult child had died. She was shattered, older and more anxious than I had ever seen her. She turned to walk with me, and as she did, started going all over again the details of her son's death, wondering why she did not know (telepathically) that her son was in trouble, and how fate could have been reconfigured, by just a matter of a few city blocks, so she might have come across him, drunk and very distressed, before he left to go home and take the overdose which would end his life.

It brought it all back, that punishing circling and circling around what had happened, with no relief and no end in sight, except the jolt at the end: Oh, he is dead, and nothing can ever be changed again.

If the dead do not go through purgatory, the living certainly do. We tell and retell the story of how it all happened. We have terrible jolts, when we first wake up, when we come across unexpected reminders of: Oh God, he is dead and I will never see him again. We, the grieving, feel as if we are just going round and round fruitlessly, until we exhaust ourselves, and stumble to a halt. Then the whole process seems to begin all over again.

But what we learn is that this is the very path to healing. I too had gone through that infernal circle for many months, until somehow I was released to move out into a new world, accepting the brute facts: this is what has happened, and now it is over.

Even though the death still accompanies me wherever I go, I seem to have absorbed it, so it has become part of my story, and my life. I found myself telling my friend, as gently as I could, that it was very early days yet, and the first months or years can be terrible, but with their passing, there is a growing peace, and the torment eases. One does not look for happiness, though that comes trailing too, but simply acceptance of what has happened, and with it an easing of the pain.

reviews and flashbacks

Likewise, once you know the facts surrounding the death, you will probably find yourself going over it again and again, imagining the circumstances in which the death occurred. This is normal. It allows the mind to come to terms with what has happened. If the event has been traumatic, these flashbacks are more likely to occur. Do not think of this form of imagination as threatening, but as allowing you to let in the actual situation bit by bit. In time, the flashbacks will fade, when the death has become more a part of you.

It is also normal to feel you must review the nature of the relationship with the person you have lost. Was it a real friendship? Love affair? What kind of marriage was it? Such questions may go on for a long time.

But it is important to know, and accept, that possibly some of these questions will never be answered. Such is the nature of death. A death may open up as many questions as it resolves. In the end, an ability to remain in the midst of doubts and uncertainties, without an irritable reaching after reasons, is the beginning of true wisdom. Perhaps Rilke says it best when he urges his young poet to

> be patient toward all that is unsolved in your heart and … try to love the *questions themselves* like locked rooms and like books that are written in a very foreign tongue. Do not now seek the answers, which cannot be given you because you would not be able to live them. And the point is, to live everything. *Live* the questions now. Perhaps you will then gradually, without noticing it, live along some distant day into the answer.

But often this quest can work the other way around. Instead of leaving you with open questions, reviewing your past can often bring insight. In fact, I began to think that perhaps one of the cruellest aspects of death is that one begins to understand the person you loved better now that they are dead. Clearing out personal things, reading old letters, looking back on the times you had together, you may suddenly comprehend the other's point of view or the other's difficulties and pleasures and pain in a more inclusive way.

While it seems cruel, this comprehension is also one of the gifts of death. It allows you to complete the other person's life in your mind. There may be moments when you think, 'If I'd known that, or understood that, I would have acted differently.' This kind of response is normal, but if it becomes a matter of gnawing guilt, you should talk with the dead person in your life and explain that you now understand better and ask his or her forgiveness.

imagining those who have died

By convention, society has given us images of how we, the bereaved, are now to see ourselves and how we are to picture our dead. Christians are taught that the dead survive as 'souls' somewhere in a space called 'heaven'. One might even be encouraged, for instance, to think of one's dead child as an angel. Yet such an image, perhaps helpful for some, for others may seem saccharine or simply feel false, and as such may act against an honest espression of our sorrow.

It is important, therefore, to test your actual experience against these images or models that society offers us in our need. How helpful are they? How true to our own instincts? In the end, you are the authority on your own grieving, and it is crucial that you use what you are feeling now to discover the shortcomings of what is conventionally held up as pictures or images of what death – or mourning – can be.

In the following section, I have tried to distinguish between conventional assumptions that lead to a deadening or diminishing of the actual grieving experience and, then, to contrast them to new or fresh ways of thinking about the directions in which our grieving can lead us.

dead-end: the deceased as 'gone'

Whether you believe in life after death or not, it is important that you imagine the person who is dead as someone you can still contact. At the very least, they live on in you, and it is important to ensure that that part of you does not die also.

During the first period of weeks or months, you may suddenly think you see the person you have lost, half hidden in a crowd or disappearing around a corner. Or your heart may jump when you see someone with red hair, like your husband's, or a small greying woman ahead of you in the street who looks just like your mother. These may be bad moments, but they remind you that the person you lost is still there and present in your thoughts.

Unconsciously, too, you are still looking for the person who has disappeared. One way to put this searching instinct to rest is to actually write them a letter. This should be a very private letter, which you begin and perhaps never end, but which tells the person who has died how you miss them and how you feel now. Doing this will help you feel more in contact with the person you loved and will help restore your sense of connection with them.

Dreams are also important at a time of the most intense grieving. The dead often come back to us in dreams, and what they say may be significant and helpful. Try to attend to your dreams, and keep a record of them if possible.

The writer Margaret Drabble recalls how, after the death of her friend J.G. Farrell, she woke weeping in the night after a dream. 'I saw Jim,' she reports.

> He was wearing his white suit; he was always very elegant. I walked towards him, overcome with relief, reaching out my hand, and just as he was about to take it I remembered that he was dead, and he began to fade and recede from my sight. He was untouchable. But was smiling quizzically, and was so much himself, so vividly himself … he shook his head slightly and continued to smile, as I began to cry, and he said: 'It's all right, you know, it's quite all right.'

For my own part, I remember the comfort of hearing my younger son recount, one morning after another, the dreams he had of his father who had died suddenly only days before. In the last dream, he said, his father had come to say goodbye. Because we never had a chance to say goodbye, I felt, and I believe we all felt, that he had taken this route to make sure that we knew he was OK and on his way and that he wished to depart not hurriedly, not without the usual courtesies, but with a visit in which he left with a parting blessing.

reorientation: imagining the body as a coat

When trying to explain to yourself and others what has happened, one of the simplest ways is to use the traditional Christian image of the body as a garment that has been flung off, leaving the spirit free to find its way to another life. For children, in particular, this is a helpful image for explaining one's sense of how the spirit persists when the body dies.

Outside the Christian tradition, the body has often been imagined as a chrysalis now discarded by the soul, which emerges from it to fly to new freedom as a butterfly.

Even if one believes that the spirit dies with the body, these images can still help in explaining the sense of presence that, for many, persists long after someone you love dies.

reorientation: imagining the life after

For many, religion helps to imagine an afterlife for the dead person. They are given a scenario of the dead in heaven, or paradise. How you imagine heaven is up to you. But I remember once my husband, on the way into town with the children on a sunny spring Saturday, suddenly turned to me and said: 'This is my idea of heaven – just like this – an ordinary day in which we are together and everything seems perfect.' That vision has given me great comfort. I can now imagine him as wandering around Dublin on a sunny Saturday afternoon, going to bookshops, perhaps a rugby match, then meeting a few friends for a pint.

Accounts from those who have survived near-death experiences also give comfort. They are astonishingly uniform in what they describe: a welcome into radiant light by those they have loved in life, and the sense of benign presences or presence which enfold them in an embrace of unconditional love. Each reports that after this experience all fear of dying has left them. Now, years after his death, I find myself thinking of my husband as standing in such radiance: loving – and at peace.

A priest I know says simply: I always think of the dead as being with God. This is the most straightforward way of expressing the sense of an afterlife, and, for the faithful, the most satisfactory. Even those who do not believe in a god can imagine some return to a primal unity within the universe.

These images heal us, and are true to our communal experience as human beings over many ages. It is important to allow them to help you place the one you have lost, and to remember that in an important sense they are not lost, either to you or to themselves.

imagining yourself

You are not yourself. Death has changed you forever.

We define ourselves through the people we love. We have grown within their expectations, their hopes, their desires for us. We are shaped by our shared histories. So that, when those we love die, we may feel we have lost a key to our under-standing of who we are and who we are to become.

In some sense, we have lost part of ourselves, too.

At first this will seem very threatening, as if you were rendered invisible. Or you may even feel you have changed into someone else, someone you no longer recognize.

In practical terms, it is important to remember that since everything has now changed, you will change too. The crucial thing is to try to direct this change.

One way of directing this change is to make a list of things you always wanted to do but never could do before. Even going out and buying new clothes, or making decisions about where you will spend the next holiday or how you will redo the house, or thinking about your plans over the next year or so and how they will be different – any of these will be gestures in the right direction.

More radically, you now have the freedom to imagine the new self you wish to become. What about the self you were before: before you married, before you had children, before you took that job? What about that side of your self that was put aside for all these commitments? Now is the time to consider a new direction for yourself and the practical steps you might take in future to accomplish it.

It is important to engage in this exercise. Otherwise you

Passing the Graveyard

I see you did not try to save
The bouquet of white flowers I gave;
So fast they wither on your grave.

Why does it hurt the heart to think
Of that most bitter abrupt brink
Where the low-shouldered coffins sink?

These living bodies that we wear
So change by every seventh year
That in a new dress we appear;

Limbs, spongy brain and slogging heart,
No part remains the selfsame part;
Like streams they stay and still depart.

You slipped slow bodies in the past;
Then why should we be so aghast
You flung off the whole flesh at last?

Let him who loves you think instead
That like a woman who has wed
You undressed first and went to bed.

Andrew Young

will simply find yourself trying to accommodate the roles others now imagine for you. While not meaning any limitation on your own life, many will make assumptions about your new role as widow or widower: for instance, that your life is 'empty' and needs to be filled; or, conversely, that you are now going to devote your life to finishing the work of your spouse or pledging yourself to worthy causes. Harmless or conventional as these assumptions may seem, they will constrict you in your search for a new life and therefore should be resisted.

Yet formulating a new life at this stage is also very difficult, as the initial stages after a death are often bewildering. In my new status as widow, and while in the process of trying to construct another life for myself, I was constantly asked to fill in forms that asked whether I was 'single' or 'married'. I found this difficult because I still felt married, and still wore my wedding ring; but, in fact, I was now legally single.

Pronouns were also a problem. What do I do about 'our' children, who had now suddenly become 'my' children? If I used the singular, people mistook me for a single mother (which I was now but had not been) or a divorcee, which I emphatically was not. 'Our' house and 'our' bed only gradually and self-consciously became 'my' house and 'my' bed, but even that pronoun, many years after, does not sound right.

In time, the pronouns settled down. But it was only when I was able to accept my new status – as a woman on my own – and began to imagine how I would now wish to live, that I was able to come to terms with what had actually happened to me.

The aim of grieving is acceptance of death, which entails an open and honest encounter with what has happened to us.

We cannot imagine another life for ourselves until we have acknowledged the fact of death, and tried to construct a narrative surrounding it that is true to the experience itself.

Although such a narrative begins with fact, it will not end there. Constructing a new life will involve a radical act of imagination in order to forge another kind of narrative. This new story may involve our account of what we think happens to the dead – as well as what will happen to us – in this, a future life. Although this is a fictive universe, the very act of imagining such a narrative will allow us to find some peace and order in the chaotic and disruptive events set in motion by death.

The Grandmother

Here it is three years since my grandmother died
– That old woman – there at her funeral,
Parents and friends, everyone was in tears,
From sadness that was bitter as it was real.

Alone I wandered through the house, bewildered
Rather than shocked; after, when I drew near
To her coffin someone did complain of me
Finding me neither beside myself nor in tears.

Noisy sorrows are quickly over and done:
Many other emotions, three years later,
Complete change – whether for good or ill –
Have washed the memory of her from their hearts.

I, I only, dream on and weep for her
Often; three years later, taking strength
From the passage of time, like letters cut on bark
Her memory, too, deepens as time lengthens.

Gérard de Nerval

three: lost in loss

feeling lost

Chaos often follows the first impact of a death.

During the early days, that chaos will tend to be organized by the rituals surrounding the dead: the gathering of family, perhaps a wake, a funeral. But when the funeral is over, the world may seem to be falling apart.

A death, even a gentle and expected death, involves enormous disruption. Emotionally it may seem like a disaster. Sometimes that sense of disaster does not hit suddenly, but gradually. As the days and weeks go by, the change that is a death will inevitably involve other changes, so they accumulate in what seems like an avalanche, or a landslide.

It is important during this period to tolerate a certain amount of chaos. Expect to feel out of control. Death is a reminder that we are not in charge of our lives. Try to accept that: and also to trust that there is an order, somewhere. The sun will still rise, the morning will come. People will still need to be fed and to sleep. You are among them. Of course, that order itself, which is the order of the ordinary universe, may well itself seem offensive in the face of the terrible violence that is a death.

Try to live with this contradiction, and remember that it is just this commonplace order, and the demands of everyday life, that will draw you back into it, and help you heal.

disordered thinking

Just as a death brings practical chaos, so it also brings emotional and intellectual chaos. In encountering a death, we are facing an event which challenges every sense of order available to us, including our certain certainties and the very words in which we voice them.

You may find you do not wish to speak, and that the words other people say seem hollow. Death has a way of emptying out words, and putting them in quotation marks.

You may find you are no longer certain of things of which you once seemed sure. The words of religion may also begin to seem like a mere formula and the words of consolation flimsy or even a sham.

Or you may go to the opposite extreme, and clutch at words or formulae that once might have seemed empty. Death gives words this resonance, so that we can go beyond them. The very capacity which at times makes words ring hollow may also now make them ring like a gong. A simple phrase or note from a friend may be so significant that you carry it with you every-where, as a kind of talisman.

On the other hand, even *you* may know that you are clutch-ing at straws. I found this in my own experience. After my husband's death, I kept a letter from one of his friends, a letter which praised my husband warmly and then went on to pro-pose a visit, saying he would like to meet his children and tell them what an exceptional person their father was. I looked at this note every day. It represented real consolation, because it told me my husband was valued, and reminded me of the wonderful person he had become.

But, gradually, I realized I was also building hopes on it. This note was from an older man who had never married. I began to have fantasies that he would visit, and then perhaps invite me out, and one thing would lead to another, and there would be another man in my life. Even though I knew it was absurd – and even pathetic – I allowed myself to fantasize this way. It seemed harmless and gave me comfort.

Then one day a note came saying he could not visit after all; he had needed to go in to hospital with an urgent heart con-dition. I was devastated – for a whole day. Then I relegated the fantasy to where it belonged: to the small things that had given me comfort and carried me through some bad weeks, and I put it away, among the other letters of consolation.

Be prepared for some crazy thoughts. Be aware they may not match what people call reality, but trust that in time reality will correct them.

As you will find, nothing is quite what it is supposed to be any more. If that reduces you to despair, it is also grounds for hope.

guilty but insane

In Irish legal language, when someone commits an act for which they cannot be held responsible because of their state of mind, there is a provision for declaring that person guilty but insane. While the parallel is obviously not exact, those who are bereaved may feel guilty even while they know that their sense of guilt is highly irrational.

Such guilt is common to grieving and is, in fact, embedded in the language attached to loss. As Oscar Wilde has one of his characters quip: 'To lose one parent may be regarded as a misfortune – to lose *both* seems like carelessness.'

What is at stake here is an exaggerated sense of personal responsibility that haunts our world. Because death is hidden, it seems unnatural, uncommon. Therefore we wonder what *we* have done to cause it to happen or what *we* could have done to prevent it.

'To lose' someone 'seems like carelessness' because it implies that, if we had looked after them or done the right thing, they would still be with us. Often people die in situations where there may be ambiguity about what might have happened if things had played out differently. Would your father have survived his heart attack if you had known the simple resuscitation technique called CPR? Would your brother have avoided the car crash if you had persuaded him to go into an addiction centre for his drinking problem? Would your wife have taken an overdose if you had managed to persuade her to get specialist help for her increasingly obvious depression?

The answer almost always is 'no': nothing you could have done would have made that difference. Or, even in the remote possibility that some action of yours would have prevented tragedy this time, there is always the next time – the next heart attack, the next drinking disaster, the next suicide attempt. We can only do what we can do, and there is often a kind of inevitability about the way people die. But this is hard to accept because we are each brought up in this world with a code of responsibility so strict it holds us accountable for practically everything that happens to us in this life.

We are also brought up with a rather naïve version of the nature of causation. If this and that one thing had happened, we are taught to think, then he or she would not have been dead.

In fact, the world is more complex than we would like to admit. When someone dies, it is usually the case that no one thing or action would have made a difference. Furthermore, to think in this way is not fruitful. It will add to the pain of your grieving and certainly delay or deflect the necessary acceptance which will ultimately bring you peace.

There are other kinds of guilt which become mixed up with grieving. It is possible that, although you knew someone was dying, you were prevented for practical reasons from going to say goodbye. I have in mind a young Chinese woman in the United States who became ensnarled in visa problems which prevented her return in time to see her dying grandmother, who had raised her as a child when her mother was abroad studying. Her grief was doubly painful for the punishment she inflicted on herself, even though nothing could have been done to move the bureaucratic process any more swiftly.

Then there are those who simply cannot bear to say farewell nor are able to find the resources to see their loved parent or child or friend over the threshold. In such circumstances, you have only one choice. If you have reached the limit of your ability to cope or if you feel you cannot bring yourself to be with the person who is dying, then you must try to understand and forgive yourself – just as he or she would surely forgive you. Try not to compound your pain by blaming yourself for things simply not in your control.

It is hard to do so when we operate in a world in which the very language we use tends to implicate us in the death of the person for whom we grieve. To use the active verb 'to lose', as in 'to lose somebody', implies an action on your part which has brought about this result. Try to be on guard against this verbal trick, as well as becoming conscious of other common assumptions which may hinder your actual grieving.

Surprised by joy – impatient as the Wind
I turned to share the transport – Oh! with whom
But thee, deep buried in the silent tomb,
That spot which no vicissitude can find?
Love, faithful love, recalled thee to my mind –
But how could I forget thee? Through what power,
Even for the least division of an hour,
Have I been so beguiled as to be blind
To my most grievous loss! – That thought's return
Was the worst pang that sorrow ever bore,
Save one, one only, when I stood forlorn,
Knowing my heart's best treasure was no more;
That neither present time, nor years unborn
Could to my sight that heavenly face restore.

William Wordsworth
(on the death of his daughter, Catherine)

what others do not tell you about grieving

One common blockage to grieving openly is the assumptions of others as to what mourning actually involves. Here are a few observations on the discoveries you will make when you encounter sorrow.

grief is not what you expected

Grieving is unpredictable. It is also complicated. While grieving, you may experience unexpected emotions. You may find yourself feeling anything from anger to relief, to a devastation so complete you are not capable of feeling at all. You may become disturbed by the intensity of your feelings and unexpected shifts across the emotional spectrum. There will be times when you will not feel in control of what you feel.

Try not to become too concerned; this is all typical of grieving. Observe – and accept – what is happening to you. You are not going mad. You are not crazy. It's just that grieving does not follow a set pattern. Just as death is a disruption of our illusion of control, so grieving itself does not have a script.

It is also possible that you may find that your grieving, or swings of mood, disturb others as well. Those who have been through it know that grief is this way, particularly early on. Try to trust what you feel and not let others tell you what is appropriate and what is not. Because modern society is so poorly prepared to help you with your grieving, there may be little communal experience about what it entails. The following is a list of things you should know about grief which people will not necessarily tell you.

grief is not one emotion, but many

There is no one feeling called 'grief' which you can pull out at appropriate times. Anger, for instance, is a common reaction to a death – even though anger is not considered an 'appropriate' emotion. At occasions such as wakes or other informal gatherings honouring the dead, people may seem to be behaving in an unsuitable way, laughing, for instance, or telling jokes. At such times it is important to remind oneself that nothing in grieving is 'inappropriate'; we all grieve in different ways at different times, and laughter is as much honour to the dead as tears.

At other times, people may be concerned that they feel very little or nothing. They need to be reassured that, in early bereavement particularly, sheer disorientation and exhaustion are more common than sorrow. Sadness comes later.

While grieving, you are also capable of holding completely contradictory emotions or thoughts in your head: thinking at one moment, 'Oh, how could she just die on me like that?' and, in the next, 'If I'd only got her to that check-up on time, she would still be around.' Don't be too alarmed: grieving is a complicated process. There is nothing wrong with having contradictory thoughts or feelings at the one time; indeed, some would consider this state the very wellspring of the creative instinct.

Remember, in your grieving: you are under no obligation to be rational or even emotionally consistent. Death is itself a great irrational, like love. We cannot understand it with our mind; we can only comprehend it as our whole being comprehends it, with every instinct and resource of what we call body or mind or soul. In the presence of this great event, your only obligation is to attend to the feelings and thoughts as they come and go and to observe them openly and honestly, so that the full value of this extraordinary experience will not be lost on you.

grief is exhausting

The emotional impact of a loss can be devastating. Apart from dealing with the practical disruption it entails, there is the emotional chaos – not only yours, but that of others too. Put this together with poor sleep, poor appetite, and unanticipated demands of all kinds, and it is not surprising that those who are grieving often feel exhausted.

Over the long haul, once the initial disruptions settled, I came to recognize grieving itself as a form of exhaustion. In the early times, I thought of it as a kind of internal haemorrhage, as if I were crying inside, and the tears were blood – but no one could see it, because it was internal. When this feeling became acute, I would try to get away for a very quiet day, in which I could have silence and perhaps some daytime sleep, to compensate for the energy that seemed to be ebbing out of me. This strategy almost always worked.

grief is very much like fear

Grieving is a visceral reaction to threat. A death is inherently threatening in so far as the death of someone you value entails your death as well. Part of you dies, too. The part remaining also knows, intimately now, that it too will die. Because grief is so very much like fear, it is important to look at it steadily: to face the fear squarely and try to understand what it entails. To do otherwise is to live a life of terminal anxiety and denial.

anxiety is a widespread reaction to death

Everything in your world has been turned upside down. The assumptions you are used to making no longer hold. The person you are used to having by your side is no longer there. The person you are used to thinking of as being yourself doesn't feel as if it is there either.

It is as if the compass to your world has gone awry and the needle is swinging around and around aimlessly. Perhaps it might be useful to recall that the only time the compass does this is when you stand on the North Pole. You are at your North Pole: death brings you to the central axis of all human experience.

Expect this anxiety. Understand it as a transitional loss of orientation that will right itself in time. Try not to be too anxious about the future and actively pursue exercises, such as yoga, qigong, and meditation, which will help you to control anxiety and accept the chaos around you. If you are yourself centred, it does not matter if, elsewhere, the centre does not hold. For the present, living from your own centre is the best guarantee that you will be able to reorient yourself in time.

grief ambushes you

Grief is ruthless and opportunistic. It will seize an opening at a time you least expect it. When you find yourself driving past the hospital where your wife died. When you suddenly come across your lover's letter or your mother's laundry list. When the dentist rings to confirm your dead husband's dental appointment.

Sometimes the triggers are obvious. If you anticipate a bad moment, try to find someone to be with you to soften its impact, or try to think of some other tactic which will ease the inevitable pain.

Sometimes, however, simple physical exhaustion or emotional vulnerability will allow grief to seize an opportunity to overwhelm you. For this very reason, you must seek to stay as physically well as possible and to take action to guard your spirit at times when you will feel especially vulnerable, such as holidays, anniversaries, birthdays, or gatherings in which the person you loved would ordinarily have participated.

grief never really goes away

As you are already beginning to learn, anything can trigger renewed grieving and there is no time frame for a grief-reaction. Even years later, you may find yourself in tears over some suddenly recovered memory. At first you may think that this reaction means you are going 'backwards', that you will never 'recover'. It is not useful to think this way. Try instead to recognize this renewed grieving as a positive sign, that you still love the person you lost, and that they are still in that sense alive to you.

Time possesses a different quality for the grieving. A moment may be recovered in an instant, even if it is years past. Grieving lives in an eternal present, which defies the ordinary measures of the calendar and the clock. It is a testament to the continuum of the spiritual life, and of the sustaining power of our capacity to love.

having been through it before doesn't necessarily make it any easier

If you have already lost someone, people may assume that when someone else close to you dies, you won't feel the subsequent death as keenly. This is rubbish. If anything, another death can hurt even more: it is like a blow to an existing wound. That you may be able to cope better with the practical details, because you have an idea now of what to expect, does not necessarily mean it will be any easier to live through emotionally.

If you have had a number of deaths in short succession, you might seriously consider counselling or other supports. For losses can accumulate, particularly if there has been no time to heal, and your resources may be depleted. Protect yourself by seeking outside help or the wider support of friends and family.

strategies for grieving

What is clear from the above list is that others may feel as lost as you do in encountering death. If the territory is not new, neither has it been accurately surveyed, and the maps that exist are simply out of date. They are pointing you down roads which are dead-ends and towards destinations that are deserted villages. What is needed is a new series of routes that will help you find a way of your own towards a new life. Below follow some suggestions for finding your own path and avoiding routes which will lead to cul-de-sacs in your grieving.

dead-end: just letting it happen

If you are fortunate enough to be able to anticipate a death, then you are less likely to just let things happen. Instead, you will have time to plan, perhaps with the loved person who is dying, for what lies ahead.

But in the case of a sudden death, you may just feel as if you had been run over by a large truck – that you cannot possibly cope – and, in any case, your spirit is so crushed that you do not wish to even try to cope. Perhaps you feel just like lying there and letting others take the necessary decisions. After all, what does it matter any more? You have lost perhaps the person you love most in the world – what difference does anything else make? What else counts?

The answer is that it can make every difference. It can make a difference to you and to others. If you can now find it within yourself to make choices as to how you will honour the one you have lost, it will also make a difference in the way you grieve. For the way you honour that person will also be the way you honour your own grief and the others around who now share it.

reorientation: asserting choice

You did not choose this death. The one who died did not choose to die. In this sense, death takes away the illusion of choice, of our endeavour to make the world conform to the dictates of our will. Yet, in the presence of death, we do not have to resign ourselves entirely to living in a world out of our control.

Death is other. And yet it is important in your grieving to make this death yours and, by so doing, to bring it into the middle of your world, thus giving it a shape and a significance.

Death tells us: You have no choice. You will die.

One can reply: Even in the way we climb the scaffold, we have a choice.

You may feel devastated. You may feel that the power to choose, and therefore the power to control, have been taken away from you by death. But by asserting choices in a world where you feel you have no choice, you will not allow death to dictate how you respond.

Therefore, seize what opportunities you have to make decisions, however small. Give yourself time to consider choices about how things will happen, if you can, postponing arrangements for a few days. Arrange as much of the funeral as you are able. Choose the music, the readings, the prayers and the speakers. Decide whether you wish to have a wake or other gathering and what form it will take. Dictate the obituary and re-read it carefully. In time, design the gravestone.

All these decisions will bring consolation, in the sense that you are exercising a creative response to your loss. These will be the first of many.

dead-end: acting to stereotype

When someone close to us dies, we are reminded that we are not in control. In life we are often assigned parts that we would not have chosen: being bereaved is certainly one of them. Not only is it a part you would never have wished to play, the script is terrible.

Of the stereotype of the widow I can speak with conviction. Widows are supposed to be objects of pity. As a bereaved person, you will certainly become so. Beware: being an 'object' is just what pity reduces you to. You will play into this script if you begin also to feel pity for yourself. True pity may feel like a moment of comprehension, both for yourself and for others; but if sustained, it will certainly become degrading.

This is the way one Chippewa woman put it:

> Sometimes I go about pitying myself,
> And all the time
> I am being carried on great winds across the sky.

Try to remember: However others may see you, you are greater than your grieving. You are still the self you always were. And now you have a chance to become more than even that: somebody who has touched the very centre of human experience and found that, in so doing, you are forever changed. You have entered a larger world. Do not subscribe to the notion of yourself as 'poor' or as someone to be pitied. Grieving does not impoverish; it enriches. Do not think that because this has happened to you, you are now not in control of your life or of the part you are to play in it. This is the moment when you get to rewrite the script, and defy the dreary expectations of others.

reorientation: tearing up the script

Others also grieve with you. Like you, they too will feel lost and disoriented; they too will feel threatened. The loss of control implied by death is very disturbing, particularly to those who have invested heavily in the values of permanence and control.

For these reasons, you may find that they want a script – in fact, may even expect you to play a part and come out with the right lines at the right moments. For instance, they may ask repeatedly, 'How are you?' For those who know the script, this is a prompt for the expected line: 'I'm doing just fine'. To answer in this way is simply to play into their denial of the realities of the situation. So I found myself replying: 'Terrible. What do you expect?'

Others may go even further, insisting implicitly or explicitly that there will be, at the end of the play, a predictably happy ending in which you 'recover' from or 'replace' your loss.

To the question: 'Have you recovered yet?' I trained myself to reply: 'I don't think anyone ever recovers from something like this.'

You do not have to sign up for a part in their play. Tear up the script. Abandon the performance. The show doesn't have to go on. You are writing a new scenario, in which the lines are your own lines, true to you. And your part will be the one you – and not others – dictate.

Meanwhile, don't accept the second-hand lines you are handed. Here are some of them:

time will heal
The mere passage of time will not 'cure' grieving nor by itself allow you to heal.

It is opening yourself to the work that true grieving requires – namely, an honesty and a radical reassessment of your own life – which, in the end, will enable you to reach some sort of acceptance and allow you to move into a new life.

you will recover
What people mean by this is that you will some day 'get back' to the place you were in before tragedy struck. You will not ever get back to that place, and therefore it is best simply to say to yourself, 'Though I will never recover, I will be able to start a new life which will in many ways be quite different from the one I had before.'

you'll have another baby/marry again – or, isn't it lucky you have another child?
To make a remark such as this reveals that the speaker has no idea of what loss – or love – entails. To love a person is to understand that person as unique, and therefore irreplaceable. People who consider these words comforting are those who operate along the principles of factory assembly-lines, in which each part is identical and therefore replaceable.

Do not even try to explain; those who speak such words can only learn their barrenness by experience.

be strong
This is an empty imperative, designed to relieve others of the responsibility of supporting you. It means, 'Be strong, because you are going to be the only support you have, so you had better be up to it.' This at a time when you are barely able to stand or sleep or eat. Some comfort!

keep busy
This is the worst of all practical advice, since 'keeping busy' will rob you of the time and energy you need to devote to grieving/remaking your life. In this sense, 'keeping busy' is as bad as getting drunk or taking sedatives.

At the same time, a commitment to a job that involves getting out of the house, making appointments, meeting deadlines and associating with people who are absorbed in the larger world is a good thing and not to be abandoned – as long as it allows you sufficient energy to cope with your grieving. If it does not, seek to reduce work hours to a schedule that is realistic, and allows for poor concentration, poor sleep, and the present overwhelming need to reorganize your life.

it's God's will
If you are a practising believer, then you might find such a statement acceptable (though many believers would not). But you may also discover that you have begun, or even intensified, a quarrel with God over his intentions. For many, this is the start of a period of passionate questioning which may lead to a deeper and more comprehensive spirituality.

For those who do not believe, such phrases are at best pious nonsense and, at worst, offensive. Many who are grieving find themselves at odds with orthodox, organized religion. Inevitably, they are embarking on a long spiritual journey. For these, rejecting such statements as too easy throws them into a mode of questioning that begins a larger process, of re-evaluating the grounds on which they have previously lived their lives.

it's all for the best

A remark so presumptuous one can only greet it with a silent stare.

Yet: there are circumstances when one can think such a thing. I remember one grieving man who told me that his wife was suffering so much in the last stages of terminal cancer, he went to the hospital chapel to pray for her to die. When he returned to the ward, she was dying. He never forgave himself.

There are times when the dying, and those who are helping them over the threshold, see death as a friend. Because we are so invested in 'keeping' people, we feel guilty for such a thought, but we should not feel so. Thus: we, the grieving, might find ourselves saying, with justification: 'It's all for the best', or 'It was a merciful release'.

But this is for *us, the grieving* to say. To have it said to us is, at best, an outrageous presumption; at worst, one can only acknowledge that the speaker is one embalmed in his or her own complacent self-satisfaction.

it's not the end of the world

However true as a matter of fact, this sentiment runs contrary to everything the grieving feel, which is: 'Well, it's the end of my world, and that's the only thing that counts right now.'

worse things could happen

Grief is unique, as the person grieved for is unique. And everyone grieves in their own way.

Sometimes, in an effort to understand their grief, bereaved people take to comparing their loss with that of others. This is a very bad mistake.

I well remember the shock when a friend of mine, who had just lost her husband, turned to another friend who was visiting and said: 'Well, it must be worse for you. You never even found anyone.' The friend who had come to console, left wounded. I suppose what was being said was perhaps a version of the old adage: 'It is better to have loved and lost, than never to have loved at all …' But in these (and perhaps all circumstances) comparisons are odious. At the very worst, they only remind others of their own unresolved sorrows.

Do not accept false comfort. Gently but firmly turn it aside.

Do not accept that you are 'poor' because of your experience.

Grieving need not impoverish, unless we follow the dreary scripts handed to the bereaved. Rightly understood and honestly encountered, if we take this chance to assert choices where we can, grieving can be one of the most intense, rich and empowering experiences within this life.

6. How Are You?

When he asked me that
what if I'd said,
rather than 'very well',
'dreadful – full of dread'?

Since I have known this,
language has cracked,
meanings have re-arranged;
dream, risk, and fact

changed places. Tenses tip,
word-roots are suddenly
important, some grip
on the slippery.

We're on thin linguistic ice
lifelong, but I see through;
I read the sentence
we are all subject to

in the stopped mouths of those
who once were 'I',
full-fleshed, confident
using the verb 'to die'

of plants and pets and parents
until the immense
contingency of things
deleted sense.

They are his future
as well as mine,
but I won't make him look.
I say, 'I'm fine'.

Carole Satyamurti

four: a world without maps

In accepting the centrality of what has happened to you and in asserting choices in the midst of a situation that is largely beyond your control, you are appropriating what is essentially a terrible and impersonal event and making it part of yourself.

In common with other central life events, grieving is a universal human experience – but it is also uniquely personal. Thus it is important, through your actions, to make your grieving your own.

To make grieving your own is to accept it. To make grieving your own is to make choices that integrate your loss into your life in ways that help make it meaningful. To make grieving your own is to discover new ways of imagining your world and the place you now have in it.

One way of making grieving your own is to resist taking on other people's models of what grieving entails. Here are a few of the more damaging:

dead-end: the stages of grief

A famous doctor once defined what she calls the 'stages of dying'. According to Dr Elizabeth Kübler-Ross, these include the following: denial, anger, bargaining, depression, and acceptance.

Others who did not have her subtlety turned these 'stages' into a progressive model, and applied it to those who are grieving for the dead as well as for the dying.

But even experienced doctors will tell you only a small fraction of those who actually know they are dying (maybe about ten per cent) will follow these stages in this order. And it is highly doubtful how helpful the definition of these 'stages' is for those who are actively grieving.

Where Elizabeth Kübler-Ross is valuable is in the acknowledgement that such apparently 'inappropriate' feelings as anger may feature vividly in a response to death.

But where this model fails badly is in implying that there is some reliable progress in the process of grieving. On the contrary, the grieving person feels that the 'stages' are all mixed up, come in no predictable order, and reoccur in an unpredictable manner.

To adopt this model for grieving will compound the sense of anguish, for it feels like failure if you are not even grieving 'properly' and according to plan.

reorientation: going in circles

More helpful is to ditch anything to do with 'stages' or the notion of 'progress' as linear and predictable. Grieving is individual. It has its own modalities and its own schedule depending on the person who is grieving. For this reason, it is important that you try to attend to your own particular way of grieving, for it will bring out those qualities which alone make you yourself.

At first your responses may seem chaotic. If you are disturbed by this, try to remember that it is entirely normal.

Yet, if you keep an account, however briefly, of your experience, you will find over time that it has an order of its own.

Perhaps the nearest model would be cyclical, a process in which your whole being seems to circle again and again around this, the crucial event of your present life. Your emotions too will seem to be circling – not always in predictable rounds, but in routes which return again and again to the same central core of your experience.

As a pattern of activity, going in circles is not really respectable in our world. It seems to denote futility, since our current notions of life and purpose all involve straight lines. We talk of 'progressing' towards certain goals; of finishing school or university; of climbing the career ladder; of laying out our lives as if they were railroad tracks. In doing so, we ignore the basic model of our natural environment: that of the cycles of day and night, the yearly turning of the seasons, and the larger cycle of experiential life. Human life can be narrated in such a way that 'development' and 'progress' are important terms: but only

The Five Stages of Grief

The night I lost you
someone pointed me towards
the Five Stages of Grief.
Go that way, they said,
it's easy, like learning to climb
stairs after the amputation.
And so I climbed.
Denial *was first.*
I sat down at breakfast
carefully setting the table
for two. I passed you the toast –
you sat there. I passed
you the paper – you hid
behind it.
Anger *seemed more familiar.*
I burned the toast, snatched
the paper and read the headlines myself.
But they mentioned your departure,
and so I moved on to
Bargaining. *What could I exchange*
for you? The silence
after storms? My typing fingers?
Before I could decide, Depression
came puffing up, a poor relation
its suitcase tied together
with string. In the suitcase
were bandages for the eyes
and bottles of sleep. I slid
all the way down the stairs
feeling nothing.
And all the time Hope
flashed on and off
in defective neon.

Hope was a signpost pointing
straight in the air.
Hope was my uncle's middle name,
he died of it.

After a year I am still climbing,
though my feet slip
on your stone face.
The treeline
has long since disappeared;
green is a colour
I have forgotten.
But now I see what I am climbing
towards: Acceptance
written in capital letters,
a special headline:
Acceptance,
its name in lights.
I struggle on,
waving and shouting.
Below, my whole life spreads its surf,
all the landscapes I've ever known
or dreamed of. Below
a fish jumps: the pulse
in your neck.
Acceptance. *I finally*
reach it.
But something is wrong.
Grief is a circular staircase.
I have lost you.

Linda Pastan

when we take that life in segments – concentrating, for instance, on how a baby becomes a boy and the boy becomes a man. But there the model of 'progress' comes to an abrupt halt, as the man turns middle-aged and then grows old and finally dies.

Grieving initiates us into the larger picture: nothing that death brings looks like 'progress' or 'success'. Instead it looks like 'regress' and 'failure' – unless we integrate it into the larger dimension suggested by the natural cycles of darkness and light, waking and sleeping, winter and summer, birthing and dying. 'Grief is a circular staircase.'

Yet despite modern society's bias towards the linear, as the metaphors drawn from nature imply, cycles are not themselves necessarily endlessly sterile or merely self-repeating. Thus the cycle of each year may bring new richness and depth to our responses. The circling of the mind around difficult questions often brings moments of illumination. Indeed, the circling of thought is itself a model of how thought progresses, just as the spiral is a useful model for the spiritual evolution of our lives, gathering experience as we move through the turning years from birth to death.

dead-end: 'recovery'

The word 'recovery' can be dangerous. It may even be useful to say to yourself from the beginning that you will never recover, in the sense that you will never recover the old life that was there before the death.

This may be a terrifying thought at first, but it has the merit of being true.

'Recovery' implies that you can literally go back to where you were before death intervened. But you can never go back to that life. The old life has died with the person you loved.

reorientation: recreating one's life

As long as one acknowledges that the old life has gone forever, 'recovery' can be a useful word to designate what you need to aim for.

Recently, an academic study found that forty-three per cent of people who survived a mass drowning tragedy rated it as a positive experience. These people said that they valued friends and family more, and no longer took their lives for granted. Having escaped death so narrowly, they now resolved to live each day to the full.

Your own encounter with death could have a like effect. Resolve that now is the time to change your life to fit your own deepest desires. Now is the time to revalue your relationship with others, both family and friends. And now is the time to live your life creatively, making the most of the new life that can await you in the years ahead.

There are many ways of reclaiming your life. What about the person you were before? The child you were before you grew up and entered the adult world – what happened to that person? What about the self you once imagined yourself to be? Now is the time to get back to the self that had to be put aside when you married or had children or took up that demanding job. If you have lost parents, this might be the time to try to understand your past, perhaps to write their history. If you have lost a child, this might be the time to look around to see what you might do for other children. Such losses can never be replaced, but we can allow them to lead us in new directions.

Bereavement is many things; but foremost among them, bereavement is a chance to make a new beginning. We are only rarely given a chance to remake our lives: this is one of them. In doing so, you may encounter many difficulties, not the least of them practical – you may have lost income, or a place to live, or what you feel to be the centre of your life. But it is still there, waiting to be discovered. Your work is now to find that centre and to grow the rest of your life from there.

dead-end: grief as failure

In today's world those who are grieving often feel in some vague but pervasive sense that they have failed. They have lost something valuable – in a world that values people as if they were commodities. They are in pain – in a world which equates comfort with happiness. They are disoriented and lost – in a world which values focus and progress towards defined goals. Finally, the grieving are often made to feel ashamed of their own feelings – because the world is not competent in dealing with them.

reorientation: liberating grief

Therefore it is not surprising that one of the unexpected losses during grief is that of self-esteem. This is in part due to the actual loss of someone loved, and also losses of income and status. But more important over time is the loss of one's own sense of one's self. Many of us take our value and our direction in life from those whom we love. To lose such a person is also to lose one's sense of who we are, and where we are going.

But I believe that another reason the grieving report a loss of self-esteem is the attitude society has towards those who are grieving. Modern society does not wish to acknowledge loss, nor is it well prepared to deal with those who are in pain. There is also a strange sense that somehow 'loss' might be catching – so that to associate with someone who is bereaved is to expose oneself to possible infection. Or it may simply be that people don't wish to deal with a grieving person; they literally don't know what to say to us.

The result is that the grieving feel somehow vaguely responsible for their condition – as if they are doing, or have done, something which makes society avoid them. For whatever reason, those who are grieving may find themselves marginalized or even gradually rendered invisible.

To feel in danger of disappearing is very threatening. To counter this sense of being rendered invisible, those in grief should recall that their experience is central and important. Rather than hide themselves, or the fact that they are suffering, they should assert their right to grieve, in public as in private, and according to their own condition and schedule.

If you find you have been thrust aside or made to feel ashamed for your present state, it is time for you to fight back. Grieving for the dying and the dead has its own fury, as the poet knows.

The Grief Liberation Front

In becoming bereaved, you will find you have inadvertently joined an underground organization.

The world is full of invisible sufferers – those who have lost someone through any manner of catastrophes. They are

Do Not Go Gentle into That Good Night

Do not go gentle into that good night,
Old age should burn and rave at close of day;
Rage, rage against the dying of the light.

Though wise men at their end know dark is right,
Because their words had forked no lightning they
Do not go gentle into that good night.

Good men, the last wave by, crying how bright
Their frail deeds might have danced in a green bay,
Rage, rage against the dying of the light.

Wild men who caught and sang the sun in flight,
And learn, too late, they grieved it on its way,
Do not go gentle into that good night.

Grave men, near death, who see with blinding sight
Blind eyes could blaze like meteors and be gay,
Rage, rage against the dying of the light.

And you, my father, there on the sad height,
Curse, bless, me now with your fierce tears, I pray.
Do not go gentle into that good night.
Rage, rage against the dying of the light.

Dylan Thomas

invisible because society prefers them to remain invisible. In our 'happy' society, it is simply more comfortable and convenient that we not be reminded of them.

Nobody seeks to be a member of this club; but you had little choice in the matter. What counts now is what you are going to do about it. When you gather enough strength, it is time to assert your rights to grieve in a manner, and at a time, which is appropriate to you – and not to others who wish to control or sideline consciousness of your pain.

your rights as a person in grief

- You have a right to remain silent.
- You have a right to cry, any time and anywhere.
- You have a right to express your grief in ways that seem appropriate to you.
- You have a right to talk about your dead spouse/child/ sibling/parent/friend as often as you would wish and on whatever occasions you wish to do so.
- You have a right to negotiate for time out from the usual schedules and obligations, so that you may honour your grief – and heal.
- You have a right to complete your grieving in your own time and in your own way, without being subject to the 'schedules' and expectations of others.
- You have a right to assert the centrality of the experience of grieving, within your own life and as it affects the lives of others.

educating others to grief

The grieving are burdened by duties. They must discharge their responsibilities to the deceased, by arranging a funeral, a burial place, a gravestone. They must discharge their responsibilities to all the other people involved, from family to friends and colleagues. And often they must deal with the terrible burden of continuing alone, to raise children who are themselves stricken by grief, or to console siblings or parents or others who loved the person who died, and to endure a new life without the support of the person they have loved and lost.

On top of this, there is the endless succession of dry official letters and arid meetings with lawyers and other experts, as the estate is settled, and perhaps the house sold, and all the other practical arrangements are made for the things that the deceased has left undone, or left behind.

But perhaps the greatest burden that the grieving carry is that of educating others to the meaning of grief – which is nothing less than educating them to the meaning of their own eventual death.

It is a thankless task, and not one that any individual in grief would willingly assume. But it is thrust upon us by the fact that others simply do not understand or do not care to understand what those who are grieving are going through. On the shoulders of mourners falls the task of integrating the dead into the society of the living. You are now the one who understands how we die with the dead and how they are born again through us. Given the modern degradation of what grieving involves, it is now up to you to impress on others how absorbing, how passionate, how life-transforming this experience can be.

You need not seek opportunities to do this; they will happen. But you can help the process along by taking it on yourself to practise a bare honesty, not to accept false comfort, to correct firmly and openly misconceptions about your present state. Say what needs to be said and no more. If you know you are going against the expectations of others in any given situation, you might wish to explain why you are doing so. The only thing others have to know is that what you are going through is important and that you are doing it your way and in your own time.

In fact, sometimes the most important thing you can do right now is just cry. Do not be afraid of embarrassing others. If you burst into tears, you burst into tears; allow yourself to cry when and where you feel like it, without any added sense of humiliation. You are not letting anyone down; you are in grief; you have a right to cry. Make others acknowledge it. Do not add guilt about your own pain to your already terrible burdens.

Every loss is unique. Each person grieves in his or her own way.
Perhaps nothing draws as deeply on individual creativity as grief does. It is a time to rally your own resources, to use them in such a way as to express your grieving as your own, and thus to take possession of it.

Spring and Fall:
To A Young Child

Márgarét, áre you gríeving
Over Goldengrove unleaving?
Leáves, líke the things of man, you
With your fresh thoughts care for, can you?
Áh! ás the heart grows older
It will come to such sights colder
By and by, nor spare a sigh
Though worlds of wanwood leafmeal lie;
And yet you wíll weep and know why.
Now no matter, child, the name:
Sórrow's spríngs áre the same.
Nor mouth had, no nor mind, expressed
What heart heard of, ghost guessed;
It ís the blight man was born for,
It is Margaret you mourn for.

Gerard Manley Hopkins

five: transforming loss

primary losses

When someone dies, others speak of our loss. In some ways, this is adequate. We are acutely conscious of someone being missing. We may know they are gone, but still find ourselves looking for them. We may know they are no longer here, but still have the impulse to turn to them, to talk with them.

In the first days, our imagination has a hard time adjusting to them not being here and physically with us.

When it does sink in, we suffer. We think of them as lost. But it is actually we who are lost. We are disoriented. Our world has been turned upside down. Our sense of ourselves also is skewed. Suddenly we are single – and bereaved. Or suddenly we are parents of only two children rather than three. Or suddenly we are orphans, without a mother or father.

In the end, in losing someone important to us, we lose part of ourselves. When someone we love dies, we die too. So, when we grieve we are grieving not only for the person we have lost but also for part of ourselves.

collateral losses

What others may not realize, is that the death of one person can bring not one, but many losses. When my husband died, I realized I had lost a lover, and a friend. But, of course, our children had also lost a father. His family had lost an uncle and a brother. Many of his friends had lost a close companion. Other losses have more immediate consequences. If the person who died was a wage-earner, you have lost income. (Many widows find themselves suddenly without adequate resources.) You have also lost status: you have become a single person, a widow or widower. You have become perhaps a single parent, and your children are now from a single-parent home. If your spouse or parent or friend was a public figure, or important within certain circles, you find you may suddenly have lost your accustomed place in the society around you. Widows, in particular, suffer from this syndrome; they are often left isolated after the first period of mourning.

Social isolation is inevitable given our attitudes towards death. Thus the pain of grieving is compounded by other losses. Some friends drift away. Others decide not to continue the friendship.

In this situation, one of the most valuable things the grieving can do is to learn to live alone, and to learn to live with a certain degree of loneliness. It is painful, but, in drawing on our own resources, this new aloneness can give us the space to create our lives anew.

The important thing is to contain the loneliness so that it does not overwhelm. Trust to the friends who remain to help you through. In the first months, it is wise to seek a new social place which is in some sense already made: go to church, if that seems right to you; discover a group of others who are in your situation or who share your interests. This may only be a transitional measure, but it will ensure that you are not sitting at home days on end while the world passes you by.

If you feel you do not have the energy to continue with your present commitments or to seek out a new social context, it is very helpful simply to make yourself your own best company. Keep up the conversation by making daily entries in a journal. Arrange your free time so that it involves doing things that are significant and enjoyable. Allow yourself as many pleasures as possible. Get out of the house to events that you can enjoy comfortably on your own, such as a concert or a sponsored walk or a public meeting. You may discover that, going to such functions on your own, it is in fact easier to mix and talk with others than if you had gone as a couple.

Finally, do all those little things that you could not do in your earlier incarnation: sleep across the bed; eat garlic, perhaps; set your own eccentric schedule.

the shape of loss

The losses so far described can be enumerated. They are the loss of a person, or of income, or of members of a social circle.

But ultimately what is missing when you lose someone you love cannot be measured.

Some people think of loss as a kind of hole. Like the hole in the doughnut, that space is supposed to be pretty much the same shape and size all the time, in the future as it was in the past. So, in time, you can take the measure of it; it is reckonable.

But loss is not like that. Over time, the hole created by loss changes shape and size. Sometimes it seems very large; sometimes not so large. It grows with us, it changes with us. Loss is not an event that begins and then comes to an end. Loss is an event that gathers up other losses into itself and changes with us as we change, for the rest of our lives.

When my husband died, he was just out of the operating theatre. Summoned by the Intensive Care staff, I went into the hospital with David, our older son, leaving the younger, Thomas, with a neighbour. Later, I decided to have him brought to the hospital to say good-bye to his father. But when he arrived, it was evident no one had told him the news. So I knelt down before him, so as to be on the level of his eyes, and said: 'Thomas, Dad is dead. He died just after the operation.' And then I took him into my arms.

But Thomas pushed me back, and stood there, in the middle of Intensive Care, and, raising his arms to the sky, he wailed: 'Oh, Mom. He should have seen me grow up. He should have seen me married. He should have seen my children.'

Thomas was eleven. But he knew even then that loss does not go away: that every significant event of his life from then on would be shaped by the loss of his father.

We can call this shape a ghost, and in saying we are haunted by it, try to articulate how we register loss at every turn of our lives. Or we can move away from this, and simply acknowledge that loss evolves along with us, changing shape as our lives change shape, and that, in so doing, it demands recognition as an absence that constantly defines our present.

Some cultures acknowledge this. Among the Chinese in Singapore, notices appear in newspapers for ghost-brides or grooms. In placing these advertisements, the parents are following the ancient Chinese tradition of seeking an arranged marriage; but the marriages they are arranging are, in this case, for the babies or young children who have died before reaching a marriageable age. In seeking a partner for them, and conducting a ghost marriage, the parents are respecting the continued presence of their lost children within their own lives and finding comfort in their newly imagined status, settled at last in a relationship where there will be another to look after them.

Although our culture does not have any such comparable tradition, it is important that we can imagine our dead as evolving along with us, not literally perhaps as people continuing on with their lives (although that too can be a way of thinking of them) but as presences which accompany us and change forever the way our lives are lived, and the decisions and direction we now take. Everything is different, now; there is another perspective on how you live, as if you looked on life with another's eyes or were now accompanied by their spirit in whatever you do.

dead-end thinking: replacement

In modern society, when you say you have lost something (or someone), you are implicitly violating a sacred principle of the contemporary Western world: The one who has the most stuff wins.

We in the West are a society based on accumulation of things. To lose a valuable thing is to lose status. A person you love is a most valuable thing. You have lost it. You are therefore diminished.

You are responding to this judgement on a very subliminal level when you find yourself feeling guilty about the loss. In my case, there were absolutely no grounds for guilt: everyone did the best they could – doctors, nurses, even myself over the years in my role as wife. But I still felt as if I had somehow been accountable for my husband's death.

The message from modern society is: if you have lost something valuable, you are somehow responsible. If you have lost something, replace it. So you will find people telling you, within days of the funeral: 'It's OK; you will marry again.' Or to someone who has lost a child: 'You can have another baby.' Love knows what it loves is unique. Even if one marries again, or has another baby, the loved one can never be replaced. That is the nature of love. Those who do not know this will never love or be loved, because they do not understand that to love is to allow oneself to be open, always, to the terrible suffering of the possibility of losing the one we have loved.

reorientation: compensation

Some of the losses which come with the death of a spouse are unexpected. One which I found the most difficult is that, after almost thirty years of a close marriage, suddenly no one touched me.

It had really nothing to do with sex – I would not have had the emotional energy for anything so overwhelming. What I missed was the physical expression of affection: the arm around the waist, the casual caress, the husbandly hug. My children were teenagers, both boys, and understandably too self-conscious for such expressions of affection. But we did take to giving each other group hugs on difficult occasions. And we had a dog; he used to sit on my lap and lick my hand; it was immensely comforting. If I had been alone at the time of my bereavement, I would certainly have considered getting a companion animal – as another presence to care for, as another living thing to touch, and to love.

It is hard suddenly not to be touched. Another in my situation told me that he went for a weekly massage – that even being stroked by a stranger made a big difference.

On a larger scale, there is a natural desire to work against the loss, to make something else happen that balances out the pain and emptiness ushered in by absence. I tried to think for the time ahead of something that I had always wanted to do, but never could carry through because of my job, or the children, or any number of reasons. These plans now became my best defence against the loss that seemed to overwhelm me at every turn. I made a list of all the things, from the sublime to the ridiculous, that I wished to achieve and never had tried to do. Now, seven years later, I see that almost every item on the list has been checked, including those that I couldn't imagine at the time as having even a hope of carrying through.

And without this death, perhaps few of them ever would have been. It is not a consoling thought. Given a choice, I would prefer to have my husband back with us again. But, because I had no choice, I was able to right the balance of loss by seeking new things to do, and thus gradually to begin to make life anew.

dead-end thinking: what might have been

A death can rob us of our past. It can also rob us of a future. With our partners, we would have planned for that next holiday, or hoped for that promotion at work, or had certain ideas about how we were to spend retirement. With children, we have planned a future, not only for them, but for ourselves. Now all that is gone.

The word 'bereft' comes from 'reave' – originally meaning to be robbed. Many grieving people feel robbed of their plans, their hopes, their expectations when someone close to them dies. They are often mired in bitterness and anger at what has happened to them. They feel like victims of some terrible violence.

It is a natural, and perhaps inevitable reaction, particularly to a sudden death. But it is important to move on from bitterness, or it will wither the spirit. The most effective way to move away from bitterness is to begin to construct a new future for yourself, and adequately to honour the past, for what it was. Becoming bitter is understandable; what has happened to you is cruel and arbitrary. But it has happened. It is time to reckon the losses for what they are. To accept what has happened – simply as something that has happened – is the condition for moving on.

desert island risks

Loss can maroon us. Absorbed by our own pain, and perhaps feeling abandoned by those around us, we can decide we are just going to wither away on our desert island. The world seems so indifferent to our fate, and escape so impossible.

In fact, escape is almost entirely a question of your own initiative. It is true that you are now isolated and that you are in a place which, for some people, is not even on the map. But at a certain stage, it is up to you to let them know you are there and you want to get off – or at least have some company in your splendid isolation.

You will know you are ready when you begin to recognize that you are on a desert island in the first place. If, after the first months, your routine seems to be growing increasingly arid – if you do not know if you are bored or depressed or both – if you feel you will scream if no one phones: now is the time to take the initiative. Lift the phone and invite someone over. It doesn't have to be a grand dinner party; supper for two on the kitchen table is quite sufficient.

Unbind the spell. Break through the silence that surrounds you. Light the fire on the beach, and let others know you need to be rescued from your solitude. Now is the time to open up to the sound of voices, to the touch of friendship.

This is a small beginning which will make all the difference. But, remember, the initiative *must* come from you – if only because your friends may be waiting for this signal from you that you are ready to begin joining the world again.

reorientation: towards a new world

From such small beginnings, great things may grow. Of those who have been able to work through their grief, many will tell you that, out of their pain and sense of devastation, they continue to gain immeasurably.

The friends who stay become better friends. The family who endure with us become closer. But the grieving have also come to understand that they are now part of another order. Our secure world is broken open: one begins to notice suffering all around us. Now that our eyes are open, we discover a huge community of silent, invisible sufferers – who are silent and invisible because that is the way modern society wishes them to be.

Since we have now paid the price of admission – in terms of pain, a very high price indeed – we should acknowledge our new community. We have become part of the brotherhood of suffering. It knows no status, nor class, nor gender, nor nationality.

From this new consciousness of pain, much can grow. It is the very grounds of our rebirth. Look around you: there is probably not one person you encounter who has not had some particular cause of suffering. Even if they do not tell you about it, you will now be able to detect it, because you know all its signs, all its vulnerabilities.

Loss is always loss; it is immeasurable. But from the experience of loss may grow another life. To begin with, you may now have a chance to begin again. There are few opportunities for us to remake our life: sometimes a death, through its sheer devastation, can clear ground that will enable us to rebuild our lives to something nearer our most absolute desire.

There are other gains. A death forces us to deal with our lives more openly and honestly; it has a way of stripping away clichés and sentimental smoke-screens. This may be uncomfortable for those around you, but it could be the making of your own life. A certain ferocity about your experience, a refusal to trick it up or accept false comfort will allow you to encounter death as it is: the one experience necessary for us to learn how to live and to live fully and openly, with courage and even with joy.

Grieving is the beginning of a process of transformation.

It is a painful process.

To endure it, you must trust the process, and rely on your creativity to transform loss into a gift.

six: only half alive

dead-end thinking: 'survivor'

The model that most people will have of you is as a 'survivor'. This image cuts several ways. There is that terrible (now thankfully obsolete) word 'relict' which used to be applied to widows, meaning 'the remnant of the dead' or a 'residuum' – as if the bereaved had no life of their own after the death of a partner.

Many people may regard you as a 'relict': literally, a small piece of the person who died. This is particularly true of widows and even more true of widows of well-known men. Those who wished to know you simply as a way of getting close to the person who has died will inflict their grief on you – as if you did not have enough of your own to bear. They will ring you up to talk about the dead one endlessly. Or, at the opposite extreme, they may simply disappear, because their only reason for wishing to know you has now disappeared.

Others again may themselves seem to be on a death trip. They will use conversations with you to talk at length about the death that has occurred, as if nothing else about you yourself seems to matter. In the early days or months, it may not; but after a year or two, their insistence that you are a death-emblem, representing only the death of another, becomes tedious. You are much more than that; and what you are now, you are only beginning to discover.

This is survivorship in the worst sense.

Another reason why 'survivor' provides a poor model for grieving is that the word ties you to the event. It thus prevents you outgrowing it. If you are always identified as the woman who 'survived' the Holocaust, or the man who lost his wife in the Twin Towers' disaster, then how can you go on to remake your life anew? The very description dooms you to relive the traumatic event – and allows that event not only to define your loss but also any new identity you may create for yourself out of that loss.

For this very reason, it is important to insist that you are larger than the event which has now remade you – and that you are not to be defined by an accident of history. In not letting others box you into a news report, you will allow yourself the freedom to move on into another life that is larger than what has merely happened to you.

reorientation: living with the damage

There are, however, some advantages to the survivor's model, if you can use it to imagine yourself as outliving a terrible accident (and maybe indeed you have outlived a terrible accident).

Following this model, you could perhaps imagine yourself as convalescing, but in such a way that it is clear that the price of surviving will be chronic pain. Although the pain will not be incessant, nor ever as fierce as in the first weeks or months, chronic pain can be a useful model in acknowledging that the pain of grief never really disappears. It accepts the fact that grief, like the fever of malaria, say, will always come and go; that it is inside you and will never completely go away. It cannot be cured.

Consequently, you will have good days and bad days. You will need to find strategies for coping with bad days: whether it be retreating into your own special space, comforting yourself with certain things, or undertaking certain rituals (such as a visit to the grave, buying flowers, lighting candles, or visiting a particular church for a prayer). Bad days are sometimes predictable; anniversaries are days you should plan for, so that some actions can be taken to avert the worst of the pain.

But more often, bad moments are unpredictable and can ambush you. Prepare to be ambushed and accept the sudden, dreadful awfulness of impact. Make contingency plans so that you can retreat to someone or somewhere to heal. Try to keep some margins in your scheduling, so that if you are ambushed you can take a few hours or a day out to recover. The ambushes will abate with time; but at first, because they are so powerful

I Am

I am – yet what I am, none cares or knows;
   My friends forsake me like a memory lost;
I am the self-consumer of my woes –
   They rise and vanish in oblivions host,
Like shadows in love frenzied stifled throes,
   And yet I am, and live – like vapours tossed

Into the nothingness of scorn and noise,
   Into the living sea of waking dreams,
Where there is neither sense of life or joys,
   But the vast shipwreck of my life's esteems;
Even the dearest that I love the best
   Are strange – nay, rather, stranger than the rest.

I long for scenes where man hath never trod
   A place where woman never smiled or wept
There to abide with my Creator God,
   And sleep as I in childhood sweetly slept,
Untroubling and untroubled where I lie
   The grass below, above, the vaulted sky.

John Clare

and sudden, you must make provision for the unexpected assault of grief.

Another aspect of this model which has its uses is that of post-traumatic stress disorder. Sufferers often experience flash-backs, compulsive reliving of the traumatic events, sleepless-ness, loss of appetite, panic attacks. If you have lost someone with great suddenness or through an act of violence or if the loss involved scenes of terrible distress, then you may be suffer-ing from this syndrome as well as simple grief over your loss. In this case, you should seek expert counselling, for it is a well-known disorder; knowing even that much can come as a relief to some who suffer.

But even if your death was not sudden or violent, the shock can still be devastating. You do not need to add to your distress by thinking you are going mad. It is normal to experience some degree of sleeplessness, some diminishing of appetite when in acute grief. If it gets to a point where you cannot cope or your physical health is suffering, you should seek a doctor's help.

It is also common to find that you cannot undertake tasks requiring a high level of concentration. You may find that, momentarily, you have forgotten the codes for the photocopier, or that your driving is erratic. I found, to my consternation, I could not read more than a sentence or a paragraph at a time. The words were in front of me, and I could have articulated them out loud; but I simply couldn't make the effort of in-terpreting their meaning. For a university lecturer in literature, this was itself frightening – until I discovered that this is a common difficulty for bereaved people. I was also reassured that my reading ability would probably return to me slowly in time (as it has).

It is also normal to experience flashbacks of the scene of the death. You may find yourself reliving it in your mind, in slow motion, minute by minute. You will find yourself having to repeat the narrative about the death over and over to inquirers of all kinds; but this, in itself, may prove helpful in coming to terms with what has happened, as every time you go over the events, your mind will begin to accept the death as a fact, if only little by little.

If you are also prone to panic attacks, try to remember that grief feels very much like fear. Many survivors experience real and continuous anxiety. They may feel that they cannot cope, that everything is getting on top of them, that just getting through an ordinary day is a heroic task – which, for someone in grief, it often is. You have several courses of action here. Try the ordinary remedies: distraction, talking with friends, more physical exercise.

Meditation can be a great help in calming anxiety, as can a companion animal which needs attention. Yoga in particular helps keep stress to useful levels. It is very important to develop particular ways of coping with panic, so that you can nip it in the bud before it starts to take over your life. Just remember, you have been through terrible pain, terrible stress. It is a normal response to feel fear. Go with it and try to cope, despite the fear. You will come out the stronger.

dead-end thinking: suttee

When someone you love dies, you die too. Part of you has gone forever, and sometimes there is the impulse to actually die yourself as well – emotionally if not in actuality.

The notion that others die with the dead is ritualized in some societies. The most infamous example is probably the now historical practice of suttee in India, in which the wife willingly placed herself, while alive, on her husband's funeral pyre to join him in death.

This practice was an explicit acknowledgement that the wife was deemed to have no existence separate from her husband; thus, it seemed logical that she not outlast him. If, however, the widow did not choose to die with her husband, she was still bound in fidelity to the man who died. She was compelled to live a life of extreme simplicity and restriction – to become a living sacrifice if not an actual one.

The practice of suttee was outlawed by the British colonial administration in 1829 and is now effectively extinct. But its logic is perfectly clear to anyone in grief. There may not be the impulse actually to kill oneself, but there is certainly the impulse to share the pain or to give the world some sign of its existence. Among the Crow Indians, widows would ritually chop off the first joint of the little finger of their left hand. When my husband died suddenly, I was tempted to follow this example – simply because the internal, hidden pain was so great, I had no visible way of manifesting it except some sort of token physical self-mutilation. Physical pain would be a relief, I felt, in the midst of such overwhelming psychic pain.

More subtle is the temptation to indulge in a certain amount of emotional suttee, by burying oneself, emotionally, with one's spouse or child, parent or sibling or friend.

There are many ways of dying while still alive. You may seek to deaden yourself: by drinking too much, or engaging in promiscuous sex, or by feeling guilty about everything you do that brings you pleasure. You may imagine it a betrayal not to feel miserable all the time. Or you may simply wall yourself up inside your house or inside your own mind, so that you are no longer available to others emotionally.

That impulse to deaden oneself is an impulse to deaden the pain. But that pain is at the quick of your life; to deaden it in this way is to prevent you from growing from your pain.

Like actual suicide, the temptation to bury oneself alive may be an acute grief-reaction. Of course there may be periods during the early time after a death that you may not feel like living. It is too hard and now even life itself seems also pointless.

If you have thoughts about killing yourself, you should seek professional help. It may mean that the pain of grief has actually distorted and blurred your thinking to such an extent you might do irretrievable damage.

Less obvious is the desire simply to bury yourself in the past. A death may bring a fear of change so great that there may be a strong impulse to keep everything just as it was before the death. This is of course impossible, if only because the first law of life is change. Thus, to resist change is, in effect, to die oneself, or to become so withered in spirit that one can no longer engage with life. If you find, after the first year, that you are opposing any and all changes in your life, you are in danger of committing emotional suttee – and should, if possible, seek the help of others who can provide practical advice on how to cope.

freezing over

'After great pain,' Emily Dickinson wrote, 'a formal feeling comes –.'

After great pain, a formal feeling comes –
The Nerves sit ceremonious, like Tombs –
The stiff Heart questions 'was it He, that bore,'
And 'Yesterday, or Centuries before'?

The Feet, mechanical, go round –
A Wooden way
Of Ground, or Air, or Ought – Regardless grown
A Quartz contentment, like a stone –

This is the Hour of Lead –
Remembered, if outlived,
As Freezing persons, recollect the Snow –
First – Chill – then Stupor – then the letting go –

Emily Dickinson

After the initial shock of a death, and a period of numbness, the pain may descend. It may come in waves, like physical pain; or it may come in shocks, like an assault. Or it may simply seem a constant drain inside – as if there were someone crying incessantly, perhaps from a radio somewhere nearby that you can't turn off.

In such circumstances, it is best to try to attend to the pain, in the sense of paying attention to it and also in the sense that you should allow for it in as many ways as possible. Try to make yourself physically comfortable, if at all possible. Try to be with people you like, who understand your circumstances, and who will be careful with you. You are too bruised now for bruising company. Try to trust that the pain will not last forever at this intensity; that it will eventually abate and allow you time to gather your resources. Try to remember that it is a natural response to what has happened to you and, like all natural things, it will run its course in time.

After its greatest intensity, the pain eases. What happens then for some people is that a kind of grey fog seems to descend. It is as if grieving has drained the world of all its colour and energy, leaving you lost in this desert landscape. For a while, I felt as if I were wandering around the scene of some great disaster, like a fire or nuclear bombsite. Not only did everything seem grey and dead, I could almost taste the ashes in my mouth.

When this lifted, all that seemed to be left was an infinite dreariness. I went through my day mechanically, feeling little if nothing. I seemed to have no energy. Everything that I had done quickly and efficiently before seemed to take ages. I loved doing things quickly, and I love people who are quick; but instead, I seemed to be slow at everything. Sometimes even getting from one task to another reminded me of wading through a muddy bog; every step took enormous effort and concentration.

countering numbness

Thus, after the period of intense pain, you may begin to feel half-dead yourself: slow, scattered, exhausted. During this period a few initiatives may help to ease the situation:

- Try to build a margin into your life, so that you can have time for yourself, so that you have space to come to terms with the changes in your life.
- Try to get extra sleep. If you are not sleeping well, sometimes a short nap at the right moment can get you through the day. Remember that grieving feeds on exhaustion and you really cannot deal with it well if you are tired out.
- Find some exercises that will increase your levels of concentration. For some, doing something creative, such as writing or painting or anything that proves, for the moment, completely absorbing, is very helpful. For others, exercises such as yoga, which both demand and improve concentration, can make all the difference to their present status.
- Touch is important. Many people who are suddenly alone after a long relationship with a lover or spouse simply miss being touched in an affectionate way. Some confuse this with a desire for sex – but, in fact, the grieving may find sex difficult at first for many reasons. One way to counter it might be to sign on for a weekly massage at a reputable provider. Another might be to find a cuddly pet, such as a calm cat or dog, which will provide unquestioning support and warmth. Trust that, in time, you will find someone else to touch again in a caring way.
- Light physical exercise, such as walking or gardening, that gets you out of doors and into the daylight – as well as in touch with the larger world – helps immensely, particularly if undertaken every day (even for a minimum of twenty minutes).

getting stuck

Along with the numbness is a sense of being half-dead oneself. One may have the sensation of being stuck – perhaps coping well superficially but feeling numbed inside. Or you might feel that something is missing to complete the grieving process but do not know what it is or how to go about finding it.

At this point it may be helpful to sign up with a group that specializes in helping bereaved and divorced people. There are such groups throughout Ireland, the UK, Canada and the

United States. A weekend with one of them may make all the difference.

If such a group is not available, you might consider going to the different Internet websites and finding help there. One such website that seemed particularly helpful was that run by Grief Recovery, Inc., which also runs workshops for the grieving in the United States.

Working with others who are bereaved or in pain is most helpful after the initial year, when the chaos and rawness of hurt have receded somewhat and you are able to take on the experience of others. This entails a certain amount of strength and a capacity for reflection that is simply not available to those in the first weeks and months of grieving. But participating in such a group can be a watershed in understanding your own pain.

dead-end thinking: grieving as illness

At some point in the grieving process, you may consider seeking professional help. If you do so, seek help for specific problems (such as suicidal thoughts or advice on dealing with grieving children). But do not fall into the trap of thinking that grieving is in itself pathological. For most people, it is not.

There are points, however, where you may get stuck and not be able to free yourself:

- If you find yourself slipping into a prolonged depression, in which you have difficulty getting good sleep, or eating properly, or even getting out of bed, then it is time to seek help.
- If you are caught in a cycle of recurrent illnesses, then it is time to seek a doctor's opinion.
- If you have persistent and recurrent nightmares or find that you are obsessed with certain images associated with the recent death, it is helpful to get a professional opinion.

On the other hand, it is important to maintain, if at all possible, your amateur status. Resist this process becoming medicalized; rather, become, if you can, the expert on your own grieving. Observe the different emotions you feel as accurately as possible. Try to understand if they fall into a pattern. Try to analyse

how you behave in different situations and how others behave
with you. Do you find yourself moving from former patterns to
new ones?

You are yourself the authority on your own grieving. In
observing how you cope, you will be better able to devise
strategies to help you through the days ahead, and better able
to understand the resources, which are uniquely yours; and
which will sustain you as you move into a new life.

reorientation: death as a gateway

Grieving is not an illness. It is rather an experience which
initiates us into a new way of seeing things.

When you are close to someone who dies, all that it may
mean to you at first is that a life has ended, and the life you had
together has also ended. But then you come to understand that
death is more than that. You begin to realize how fragile an
enterprise life is – and how precious. You begin to question the
stock answers you have had to the big questions: Why do we
live? What happens when we die? How shall I live now?

If, in the middle of your pain and confusion, you can allow
yourself to remain open to these questions, you will recognize
that deadening or even dying yourself is not in fact a solution to
your pain. It will cause even greater grief to those around you.
It will necessarily add to the damage. After all, if one person has
died, there is no point in another person being deadened or
actually wasting away.

Thus, even in grave distress, remember: grieving gives you
a moment of pure choice. You can choose to die. Or you take the
larger risk by throwing yourself back on your own resources
and saying: This is the part that takes courage. A door has
closed. But another door has opened. I am free to choose – and
I choose: life.

reorientation: dying to the past

There is a story about Buckminster Fuller (the inventor of the
geodesic dome) who, as a young man, fell into such despair he
contemplated taking his own life. He went to the edge of a cliff
and sat there thinking of the consequences of throwing himself

over. After a great deal of thought, he concluded that, while he could not continue living as he had, he could not inflict the guilt of a suicide on those he loved. So, rather than kill himself, he decided to live life from that moment on *as if he had already died*. In that resolution he found the formula which released him from his previous life into a new and liberated existence.

We who are grieving must understand first that, indeed, we have died, and, second, that we are, by that death, liberated into a new world. We must work out our liberation, which is the hard work of grief. But living through a death gives us a rare chance to remake our life nearer to our heart's desire. We do not often have such a chance, but death sometimes gives it to us.

reorientation: how one lives again

Shortly after my husband died, I had a very strange dream. I dreamed I was in labour and that when the child was born, it was a son – and looked just like my husband in his baby photographs. It seemed such a weird dream that I put it aside for a while until I had time to make some sense of it.

As I spoke to others about my husband and began to clear out his things, deciding what to keep and what to let go, I suddenly realized that his history – that is, his life – was largely in my hands. What I chose to tell or not to tell, what I recalled or chose not to recall, these things would constitute what he was remembered by. No one living knew him as long or as well as I did. How he lived on now depended on me, and the way he was commemorated could give him life again.

I was reminded of this dream by a recent letter from a new friend, still grieving for her husband of thirty-one years. When it was clear that he was dying, she had said to her son: 'Your Dad and I have lived together so many years that I feel we have become one person. When he dies, part of me is dead too. Life will never again be enjoyable for me.'

Then her son said something that surprised her: 'Since you and Dad have become one person, then Dad will continue to live through you. Whenever you enjoy something wonderful like this blue sky [they had walked outside the hospital wards into a lovely April morning], or anything else that is beautiful, you must remember my Dad is in you and with you, and you are enjoying wonderful things together.' So, she writes, whenever she was very sad, she would remember what her son had said, and that gave her courage to overcome her deep grief.

The dead live with us, and through us. Thus acting to commemorate their memory, gives them renewed existence. A simple gesture such as calling them to mind when we see something they would enjoy allows them to remain with us, as part of our daily lives. In rejecting emotional suttee, we have rejected the option of dying with the dead. But what about the process in reverse? Could we use some phrase like 'rebirthing' to describe the means by which we consciously give the dead an extended life, in allowing them to be born again through the way we live now?

dead-end: acting to stereotype

Even while you may feel like dying yourself, or that you will never be the same again, you should remember that every fibre of your being is struggling to heal. The instinct of nature is to heal, and you *will* heal – if you allow yourself time and opportunity and you are able to avoid the ways in which the expectations or demands of others prevent or stunt your new growth.

Because of the overwhelming event that has happened to them, the grieving often may feel helpless or incapacitated or isolated and therefore perhaps even more eager than normal to fit in to the expectations of others.

This is a trap. Consider the stereotypes of the widow: poor, anxious, helpless. At best, pious and dedicated to a life alone, devoted to preserving the memory of her husband, or spoiling her only son. Who would wish to be this 'wee … cow'rin', tim'rous beastie'?

There are other stereotypes, even worse: the widow as rich, entitled, sexually predatory, who haunts fashionable parties with a view to snatching other women's husbands away from them. For the widow who finds herself grateful to be invited to a party (at last) and then treated as if she were somehow a threat, this is cruel indeed. All she wants is someone to talk with her! It has been hard enough to come to the party in the first place, and then to be faced with a Noah's Ark of complacent couples, when she must leave on her own and go to bed alone. As one widow remarked, on leaving such a party: 'I smile, and smile; but my heart is full of broken glass.'

reorientation: using the stereotype against itself

You do not have to live up to the expectations of others. You have done nothing wrong. Why should you do penance? Why should you be treated as a nuisance or a threat? You are the same person you were before you were bereaved; except now, perhaps, you listen more carefully, you are more sensitive to others' pain, and you are more appreciative of the kindness of others.

Abandon the performance. Act as you always have done. Or write your own script. If you feel like going out and buying a wardrobe of drastic black, do so. If you feel like going out and putting on your highest stiletto heels, do so.

Better still, turn the stereotype against itself. If at a party, you find yourself being nervously monitored, decide to take up the offensive. Dress to the hilt, put on your best jewellery and make-up, and when you enter the room, look around for the most attractive man in the gathering. Then go right up to him and start flirting. Usually, he will panic: 'Oh,' he will probably say, 'have you met Emily? I think you must meet Emily, she's right over there. Emily? Come and join us!' Certainly if he were spoken for, you will be informed in a matter of minutes. But – if not – you may have a very good time.

As the one left behind, you have a choice.

You can die with the person who has died. To do so is easy; it is as simple as numbing your emotions, finding ways of deadening yourself, feeling guilty if you do not feel sad, turning down every invitation that comes your way, and refusing to take part in the inevitable changes that follow a death.

Or you can choose to live. This takes courage. In the end, it is up to you. What is important is that you know that you do have a choice and that it is still possible to create a good life out of the suffering that grieving necessarily entails.

Love

*Because of you, in gardens of blossoming flowers I
ache from the perfumes of spring.
I have forgotten your face, I no longer remember your
hands; how did your lips feel on mine?
Because of you, I love the white statues drowsing in
the parks, the white statues that have neither voice
nor sight.
I have forgotten your voice, your happy voice; I have
forgotten your eyes.
Like a flower to its perfume, I am bound to my vague
memory of you.
I live with pain that is like a wound; if you touch me,
you will do me irreparable harm.
Your caresses enfold me, like climbing vines on
melancholy walls.
I have forgotten your love, yet I seem to glimpse you in
every window.
Because of you, the heady perfumes of summer pain
me;
because of you, I again seek out the signs that
precipitate desires:
shooting stars, falling objects.*

Pablo Neruda

seven: remembering and forgetting

There is a terrible moment after someone dies when you realize you no longer remember the face, the hands, of the person you loved. You might find yourself staring at photographs of your former spouse and asking yourself: Was that really you? What were you really like? And then thinking: I can't remember what it felt like to kiss you; I can't remember the sound of your voice. To forget these things seems to redouble the grieving, as if with each loss of the physical memory, you lose that person all over again.

The shocking thing about loss is that it keeps recurring in this way: it is not a once-off event, but one that keeps happening. As the actual loved presence begins to slip into oblivion, one suffers again. As he or she seems to fade from the memory of family or friends, one suffers again. When the hard-won accomplishments of that life seem now to dissipate and slip away, one suffers again. In struggling against this continual erosion, grieving renews itself, and simply accepting this continuing loss seems itself a betrayal.

Yet the work of grieving is, in part, to accept that loss is like this, while also attempting to understand what is to be forgotten and what is to be remembered. For some, this may be the work of a lifetime.

Forgetting the physical presence is inevitable; but for some, it is replaced by a new ability to see the world through the eyes of the person who is lost. Often the grieving appropriate the stance, the mode of thinking, even the occupations and preoccupations of the person they have lost. They may also seek to complete the life-work of the person who has died: to finish one of his interrupted projects, to fulfil a promise made or edit her book or arrange an exhibit of his photographs. This is a concrete way of ensuring that the loved one's life continues on into a new future.

But forgetting also involves forgiving. The first person you must forgive is yourself. You cannot help forgetting and you must resist guilt about doing so. It is part of the nature of the change in which you are now involved. In any case, remembering is not merely about physical things; it is about keeping in mind the spirit, the commitments, the passions of the person who has died.

Then you must forgive the person, above all for dying. Then for everything else. In reviewing your relationship with the one who has died, you will find that you will need to let go the hurt of episodes from your shared past, as well as the hurt inflicted by things you have discovered after his or her death. Many widows have told me about the shock of discovering mementos of other women among their husband's things. Or (perhaps worse) discovering secret debts or even secret children after his death.

Forgiving the person who died need not involve wiping these episodes from the record. Indeed, it must be acknowledged that they cannot be wiped out. But in time they can be acknowledged for what they were – mistakes, injuries, misunderstandings – and kept in memory as events but not kept in order to hold on to the pain they once involved. Sometimes people keep these injuries alive almost unconsciously, as if returning to them becomes a way of remaining close to the person who has died. Do not compound your pain in this way. Trying to place these episodes in a context where they may be accepted is very important if you are to complete your grieving.

Then there is the task of remembering. It is important that you and others around you recall the person who died – as he or she was, in every aspect of life, whenever the occasion seems appropriate. It is also important to speak of the dead as if they were living, to keep their spirit alive among you by remembering them accurately, which means that you remember them as they were in life, warts and all. Making an idealized object of the dead person does no service at all, either to the living or the dead.

Commemorations of all kinds are valuable. Here is an opportunity to exercise choice and to have the person you love honoured in an appropriate way. Writing a short account of his life, making a donation or other gift in her name, or any other imaginative gesture which marks the value of the life to be commemorated is helpful and comforting.

Remembering and forgetting is a delicate process; it is necessary to try to keep a balance. Forgetting things about the person you loved is no betrayal; it is a way of letting the person go. Try to see it also as a way of releasing yourself from a long and complicated relationship, so that you too can now go your way, enriched and enlightened by your experience.

Be assured that whatever is forgotten often returns as a form of grace, enhancing the way you now see the world. Because you grieve for the one who is lost, the world is forever different: darker, but also more intense, more radiant, more precious than ever before.

Grieving has taught you much: that everything changes, and that everything about you is the more to be cherished for the fact that one day, it too will vanish.

unhelpful strategies:

dismissing the dead

Sometimes there is a temptation when someone dies to complete the process quickly: to clear them out of the house, out of your lives, as efficiently as possible. This is a reaction of hurt – treating the death of the person you loved as if they had rejected you. In turn, you reject them. The anger infects much of what you do. You stuff all the clothes into plastic bags and leave them at the recycling centre. You burn letters. You give away personal possessions. You refuse, insofar as it is possible, to think of the dead person except as dead.

While to react angrily in this way is understandable, and even part of the expected script, it is not helpful in keeping you to the essential work of grieving, which entails working with the pain to the point where it can be accepted and valued. So be aware that being efficient at this point in the grieving process can also be highly dysfunctional.

Huesca

Heart of the heartless world,
Dear heart, the thought of you
   Is the pain at my side,
The shadow that chills my view.

The wind rises in the evening,
Reminds that autumn is near.
   I am afraid to lose you,
   I am afraid of my fear.

On the last mile to Huesca,
The last fence for our pride,
Think so kindly, dear, that I
   Sense you at my side.

And if bad luck should lay my strength
   Into the shallow grave,
Remember all the good you can;
   Don't forget my love.

                        John Cornford

forcing change

Just as clearing out precipitately may be a way of dismissing the dead, so refusing to change anything ever is a way of denying death.

What is important here is finding a middle ground. On the one hand, you must say to yourself that life will never be the same again. Death has made a momentous breach in the way you live.

Yet you may seek for months, even longer, to keep things the way they were before the death. You may not feel able to change anything, and there is no point in trying to change things suddenly when you are already in emotional turmoil.

Do not in fact change anything until you are ready.

But also do not try to keep everything the same.

If you never change anything, you cannot embark on this new life.

But change is painful and difficult.

Begin with the small things that have to be changed.

Tackle the others as they come along.

Trust yourself to know when you need to do things such as clearing out clothes or papers or a study or a studio or an apartment or a house. You will know when the time is right. Until then, it is not a crime to leave things as they are (whatever other people may say). If that special study or studio makes you feel better, leave it as it is until you are ready to make changes.

Understand that this death, and the pain that comes with it, may be in time the beginning of a new life. Be open to the possibility without forcing it.

In time, you will see that the small changes have escalated and accumulated and that, eventually, they will amount to a changed life into which you will be reborn.

cutting off communication

You may also have, during the early days in particular, a strong sense of the presence of the one who has died.

Do not shut yourself off from this feeling, but try to be open to it. If you feel like it, talk to the one who is dead. Tell them how you feel. And ask them to help you.

If you imagine the person who has died as now liberated

into a larger world when anything is possible, you will see the point of this. Many people will tell you that after someone they loved died, they had a distinct sense that they were being looked after, and that things happened for them that they had not previously thought could be possible.

reorientation: acts of completion

When someone dies, there is a great deal of unfinished business. Some of this will be actual business. But much of it will be emotional business; the ongoing transactions of a living relationship. But what many people forget is that when someone dies, a lot of hopes and dreams and expectations about the future die with them.

An important part of grieving is reaching some closure to this unfinished business, and an acceptance of all the emotional loss which has followed the loss of someone we love. To complete our grieving, it is important to follow the full arc of this loss, to record it, to acknowledge it, and then to let it go.

Here are some of the more useful acts of completion.

opening up communication:

- *writing*

  A useful way of opening contact is to write a letter to the person you have lost. Make it an open letter – don't feel you have to end it or give it any particular shape or form – just write, adding things as they come to you. It will help you to resolve many things between you, and to allow you to move on to the new life which awaits you. It helps the letting go.

- *talking*

  Most people who have lost someone they loved find themselves talking with them. This is normal, and healing; it does not mean you have gone mad. In fact, it is one of the best things you can do. The dead do not leave us because they have died. They still live on in our lives, and in the lives of our family. In our house, we refer to them as the 'dead members of our family' – and we regularly talk about

them and pray for them as if they were still among us –
which in a sense they are.

• *forgiving*

You must forgive the dead for dying. They could not help it.
You must forgive the dead for all the wrong they have done
to you, so that they can leave in peace.

You must also ask the dead to forgive you for all the
wrong you have done to them, so that you can understand
and accept the life you had together.

You must also forgive yourself for all the rage, all the hurt,
and bitterness of your grieving, in order to be released with it.

One of the lasting legacies of uncompleted grieving is
bitterness. But you must move on from the sense of outrage,
injustice, and sheer pain that this death has brought you.

Death is painful, outrageous, and unfair; but once one
moves beyond that, one can come to terms with it as something which has merely happened and, in happening,
changed your life forever.

• *acceptance*

Simply accepting the fact of a death, as well as the pain that
death brings, liberates one from perpetual grieving. But of
course there is nothing simple about accepting death. It is
the sign that you have undertaken the work of grieving and
are in the process of completing it.

• *asking for things*

One of the signs that you have moved on is that you can
relate to the dead person in your life.

In the early days after my husband's death, I asked him
to do things for us. I figured he was in a special position to
help, and I desperately needed help, so I made these
requests in an urgent, not to say wifely, fashion.

It did occur to me that this was a slightly crazy thing to
do, but I saw no harm in being somewhat eccentric, as long
as I made allowances for what others would think of my
behaviour (I simply did not tell them). Widows have a
reputation for being eccentric anyway, so I did not allow
this to disturb me (much).

What is interesting is that virtually every thing, large or small, which I asked for did actually come about, and in comparatively short order. Except for one thing. I never did win the lottery (or, at least, I haven't won it yet). When I at last had the courage, more than a year later, to tell a friend of my transworld requests, she just laughed and said: 'Well, you know, he never was much good with money!'

However odd it may seem, making these requests works for me. It makes me feel better. It focuses my mind on what I most require at the moment. And when it happens, I feel my husband is still looking after me and my family, and I feel better.

- *creating a chrysalis*
  It is hard to find a name for the comfort that comes from surrounding yourself with things associated with the dead person, but it is real and sustaining.

  At first, I thought I was the only person who put on my husband's shirt to sleep in at night. It was as if in putting it on, I had found a way to be near him. When the weather became colder, I started wearing his old sweaters. They still had a slight smell of his favourite after-shave, and wearing them made me feel as if he were hugging me. These measures were immensely comforting.

  Then I hit on the idea of sitting in his study to read. Only because it was his study, and not mine, I had to change it gradually to fit my needs. But I also moved books and other articles into that study that he had valued, so that it became a kind of sacred space where I could sit and commune with him.

  Knowing I was in a chrysalis state, I imagined this space as a kind of cocoon where I could be quiet and grow in the dark until it became the time that I had to go into the world again. It was to be the space in which I was to be transformed.

  Then I read about the woman whose husband died in the Twin Towers' disaster. She had devised what she called her 'dreaming room', a place where all that was sacred to their marriage was kept, and where she could be in spirit with her husband again. When she decided that, in her new house, she needed to do things differently, she took out her wedding dress and danced around the room for a last time before bidding the 'dreaming room', and her marriage, a final farewell.

making space for 'a dead member of the family':

rituals

These may be formal or informal, traditional or invented.

Many faiths allow for occasions for prayers to be offered for the dead. It is important to seize these occasions to remember your own special dead, as they allow others to remember them together with you.

In our family, we always mention the dead – in our usual prayers (such as grace on Sundays). On special occasions we make space for the dead in our families, making sure they are remembered among us at those times.

commemoration

As a way of honouring loss, public commemoration is essential. It also helps others to share in your grief, by extending recognition to the dead person.

Usually the first act of public commemoration after the funeral is raising the gravestone. In designing this, try to exercise your own choice about type, shape, and inscription. Even if it takes some time to get it right, remember the stone will be there for a long time and it is important to try to get it the way you want it.

If possible, at some point it is a good thing to give a gift in the person's name to some public organization with which he or she would have been associated, whether church or school or worthy public enterprise.

Private commemorations are also important. Try to organize small rituals for birthdays, anniversaries, or other important landmarks in your life together.

As in all families, you may wish also to have small invented rituals which help us to remember those who have died and which help, on important days, to keep them in mind.

Though my mother was already two years dead
Dad kept her slippers warming by the gas,
put hot water bottles her side of the bed
and still went to renew her transport pass.

You couldn't just drop in. You had to phone.
He'd put you off an hour to give him time
to clear away her things and look alone
as though his still raw love were such a crime.

He couldn't risk my blight of disbelief
though sure that very soon he'd hear her key
scrape in the rusted lock and end his grief.
He knew she'd just popped out to get the tea.

I believe life ends with death, and that is all.
You haven't both gone shopping; just the same,
in my new black leather phone book there's your name
and the disconnected number I still call.

                                        Tony Harrison

dead-end: holding on

The implicit danger of acts of commemoration is that they may become exaggerated into acts of concretion. We instinctively resist loss by trying to keep things as they are. Not some things. Everything. That way our own death lies, for the law of life is change.

We cannot hold on to anything. Not the people we love. Not our parents. Not our lovers. Not our children or even our pets. Holding on is what one does with possessions. But nothing living belongs to us, and is not ours to keep.

Once one accepts that holding on is, in fact, a law of death and not a law for living, then it is easier to identify the many ways we hold on that are in fact preventing us from now living as fully as we can.

Here are some ways we hold on:

- by resisting any change, big or little, in our lives;
- by insisting that the conditions of the old life still hold;
- by not accepting inevitable changes in our lives;
- by keeping our actual surroundings exactly as they were;
- by not clearing out, even years after a death;
- by giving our lives entirely over to the commemoration of the life or work of the person who has died;
- by now trying to control as many aspects of our own life and those of others as is possible;
- by resisting the instinct of others, such as our children, to move onward towards changes in their own lives;
- by investing heavily in artefacts or real estate or other things that seem to give an air of permanence to our lives.

The law of life is change. To hold on to people as if they were things, to try to hold on to either the dead or the living, is to deny a basic law of life – and to do so is effectively to die ourselves.

reorientation: letting go

When someone close to you dies, part of you dies too. For many of us, the first experience of death opens up what our own death will bring: a gradual slipping away of all that means most to us: our youth, our accomplishments, our friends, our family – in fact, of our whole world.

My husband's grandmother, then in her nineties, used to reply to questions of 'How are you?' by saying: 'Learning to die'.

She was of the old world. No one today would respond in such a fashion – it would upset the visitors. But of course, what she spoke is the truth. Grieving is in fact learning to die. It allows us to begin to come to terms with our own inevitable death.

To learn to die is to learn to let go. Letting go is not merely grim resignation to the passing away of our world; it is far more comprehensive than that. Letting go involves an understanding that dying is itself a significant act of giving oneself away. One gives oneself away to others – but also for others. One does not only give things, but what one can of oneself – of one's talents, knowledge, wisdom.

Thus dying, rightly carried out, is an act of radical trust, that allows imaginatively for the possibility of other lives which will continue to go on when we disappear.

But now that sense of letting go must follow us every day that is left to us. Because we now know we will die, we must be like the drunken man of the Chinese sage, Zhuangzi, who held him up as an example of how to live according to The Way, or Dao:

> A drunken man who falls out of a cart, though he may suffer, does not die. His bones are the same as other people's; but he meets his accident in a different way. His spirit is in a condition of security. He is not conscious of riding in the cart; neither is he conscious of falling out of it. Ideas of life, death, fear, and so forth, cannot penetrate his breast; and so he does not suffer from contact with objective existence. And if such security is to be got from wine, how much more is it to be got from the Dao? It is in the Dao that the Sage seeks for his refuge, and so he is free from harm.

For Christians, the mystic Julian of Norwich sums it up best in her revelations of a God who, out of 'tender love ... comforteth readily and sweetly, signifying thus: It is sooth [true] that sin is cause of all this pain; but all shall be well, and all shall be well, and all manner [of] things shall be well.' Julian knew that a key commandment of the gospel was 'Be not afraid'; her visions speak repeatedly of the need for confidence in a compassionate God who cares for his people as tenderly as a mother for her child.

What is damaged by loss is radical trust.

The work of grieving is that of acknowledging the loss and recovering the trust – by the act of acceptance of death and its accompanying pain.

eight: grieving in a 'happy' world

The modern Western world is a cruel one for the grieving. While others are making apparent 'progress' through their lives and careers, the grieving feel mired in pain. The pain goes round and round; in such a state, 'progress' towards 'recovery' seems a bad joke. In such a state, the kind of concentrated, goal-oriented activity that leads to 'success' in modern society is virtually impossible.

dead-end thinking: the obligation to be happy

Meanwhile, as well as being successful, modern society also makes us feel we should be happy. Like the many other goods that come with 'success', happiness is regarded as yet another kind of desirable consumer commodity. Thus the unhappiness of the grieving is regarded as yet another radical failure to meet the unspoken values of modern society.

reorientation: the centrality of suffering

Of course, as the above paragraph demonstrates, what grieving does is reduce many of the unspoken values of modern society to words within quotation marks: what it means to be 'happy' or a 'success' is now exactly what grieving puts under question.

When first grieving, you may feel you will probably never be happy again. Then one begins to notice how artificial happiness is anyhow. People you thought happy confess to you their own hurts and losses. With your new-found pain, you are also able to detect, almost as if by radar, the pain of others lurking beneath their professed happiness.

In grief, you might also find yourself beginning to resent

the pressure you sense to pull yourself together and start being 'happy' again. Or at least, to start acting 'happy', so as not to tax the good-will of others, who are probably also putting a tremendous amount of energy into acting 'happy', and do not need a reminder of how difficult it is to keep the performance up.

The best response to the pressure of modern society to be happy is simply to repeat the Buddhist motto: Life is suffering. As a model for human life, it probably does more to sustain us during difficulties than the vapid Western notion that the fulfilled life is one that is 'successful' and 'happy'. The Buddhist response is certainly truer to our deeper sense of what living fully entails. But like all wisdom, it is brought at a price.

For the Buddhist, that price involves abandoning all attachments: to material possessions, physical pleasures, personal accomplishments and relationships; above all to one's very ego or identity. Even death does not end this discipline, for one may go through many life cycles before one enters that desireless state which defines liberation or enlightenment.

By way of contrast, Christians understand this stripping away as a kind of suffering itself. To most of us, it comes through failure or illness or death. For some it is entered into willingly, as part of a spiritual discipline. But for all Christians suffering has a particular meaning: when we come to understand it aright, it is something we do for others. Suffering breaks down the walls within us, so that we become weak, so that we become helpless, so that we must open ourselves to others and even perhaps to that great Other whom we call God. It is the means by which we give ourselves away and allow others to give themselves to us. By this means suffering is transformed into an exchange which, for want of a better word, we may call love.

Thus to understand life does not deny happiness. Indeed, for some, it may even bring it. The way this new understanding works is the way chiaroscuro works in painting: by making the dark places darker, the places where the light falls become more radiant.

Without such darkness no places in our life would shine.

dead end: fear of change

Modern society is also badly prepared to acknowledge our loss

Yes

Now we are like that flat cone of sand
in the garden of the Silver Pavilion in Kyōto
designed to appear only in moonlight.

Do you want me to mourn?
Do you want me to wear black?

Or like moonlight on whitest sand
to use your dark, to gleam, to shimmer?

I gleam. I mourn.

Tess Gallagher

insofar as it is one heavily invested in values of permanence. The developed Western world places a huge premium on owning things, which it regards as valuable – not only in themselves, but as designators of wealth and status. Things themselves have a large symbolic function in our daily lives precisely because they endure – when human beings do not.

Because it is so invested in the values of thinghood, Western society seeks to extend its qualities of permanence to people. Thus people are urged not to 'age' – as if this were a matter of choice. Women in particular are subject to a great deal of pressure to remain young looking through various cosmetic treatments, including drastic surgery. They are asked to maintain an illusion of permanent youth, and in so doing, they embody our deepest fear of change.

reorientation: initiating change

Yet what death impresses on us is the truth that everything changes, all the time. The death of someone we love is only one of the more dramatic changes of our life. It may have been preceded by other changes (aging, illness) and will lead to more changes again.

Accepting that the world is not static, that we are all changing all the time, makes it easier to accept death: not as an offence against the natural order, but in some sense as its completion.

Thus the period of grieving is often a good time to institute some very conscious changes. You may wish to do something that will commemorate the person who died. Or something that will provide you with a new comfort. In my case, I decided always to have fresh flowers in the house. The flowers were, in part, in remembrance of my husband. But they also gave me something beautiful to look at every day – as well as reminding me of the fragility of human life.

You may consider taking up a new venture – perhaps something you postponed for years or something you always wanted to do but were prevented by circumstances. If you have nursed a sick spouse for months or perhaps years, you are now free to direct your energies elsewhere. If you have been suddenly released from the responsibilities for an elderly parent, you now have the time to devote to doing something else.

In any case, what you should try to say to yourself is: this is the end of something. But it is also the beginning. This is the time to remake your life, to make it nearer to what you would desire.

But sometimes the formulation may seem too blunt – it is too easy simply to say: this is an opportunity to remake your life. There are moments when such a formulation seems helpful, but perhaps it is better phrased in another way: that, in mourning we have, in some sense, begun to accept that through our loss we will inevitably be changed, possibly for ever. As one philosopher has put it, perhaps mourning has to do with agreeing to undergo a transformation (or should one say *submitting* to a transformation?), the full result of which one cannot know in advance.

There is losing, we know, but there is also the transformative effect of loss, and this latter cannot be charted or planned. One can try to choose it, but it may be that submitting to the experience of transformation itself means that at one level we must choose not to choose. I do not think, for instance, that one can be goal-oriented when it comes to loss. One cannot say: 'Oh, I'll go through loss this way, and that will be the result, and I'll apply myself to the task, and I'll endeavour to reach the resolution of grief that is before me.' In the process of mourning, one is subject to other forces beyond one's control so that often one starts out the day with an aim, a project, a plan, and finds oneself foiled. One finds oneself fallen. One is exhausted but does not know why. Something is larger than our own deliberate plan, our own project, our own knowing and choosing.

Thus, to make wilful or drastic changes during the first year or two is not recommended. You have waded into the sea; wait to test the undertow. When you have accepted that you are now caught up by forces larger than yourself, you will then be able to calculate how best to ride the tide that is carrying you and how your strengths will be best deployed to handle the passage before you.

dead-end: being self-sufficient

Western society also places huge value on self-sufficiency.

Western children are raised to believe in the importance of being 'independent' and 'self-assertive': effectively to act as if they were the most important person in their world and possibly (at times) as the only person in their world.

The assumption implicit in this cultural bias is that one can act as if one were independent or at least as if one's own concerns have a value prior to the concerns of others. The same assumption extends to the way most people in the West understand the world: as connected by single one-way and linear strands of cause and effect – but not as if we were radically interconnected, so that one action inevitably causes a reaction somewhere else. In the Western world, accordingly, great value is placed on the individual and his actions, at the expense of emphasizing the context which enables him to act as he does and which, inevitably, is changed by what he changes.

reorientation: everything is connected

The predictable result of the Western model is a great deal of loneliness. People tend to think of themselves as cut off from others in the ordinary course of life. How much more must they suffer from this sense of isolation if they are now grieving for someone they love.

Not all this loneliness is self-induced. Because Westerners cannot cope well with change, and thus are poorly prepared to cope with death, they tend to isolate the person in grief, if only because their state reminds them of the inevitability of change and death.

It is important to try to turn this isolation around. For many, the experience of grieving can be used as an opportunity to discover how they are connected with others. It may be that, in your pain, you will find unexpected resources in those around you. Perhaps those you had not previously thought of as friends will come forward. Naturally, you will find an unexpected connection with others who are also suffering. You will find, too, that your connection with the person who died may also still be strong. Do not resist this, but instead accept it as a testament to the interconnectedness of the world and of those who love each other.

In terms of the larger world, it is useful to try to be open to unexpected connections. Value each invitation as it comes your way: consider what thinking went into it, and the consideration it represents. Do not turn it down wilfully. All invitations are from heaven, perhaps.

Try to begin to think of yourself as part of a larger world. You are not alone. You may feel very lonely in the absence of the person you love. You may even choose solitude for a while. But try to imagine the many ways in which you are connected to others: the people who look after you every day; the people you work with; the people you meet, even in casual encounters; the people you love, even if far away.

Just as you now know yourself to be part of a world in which everything changes, you should try to consider how everything is interconnected. You do not know where this change, which is the change brought by death, will lead. Be open, be alert, and ready to accept it may bring you to places and people you have not encountered before.

When you allow yourself to become more aware of the connections between people – perhaps connections you have not even imagined before but which your grieving now discerns – try to imagine these as a kind of net which will hold you if you fall. Occasionally, like a tight-rope walker, you may fall, or even deliberately let yourself slip, to test the safety net beneath you. It is there; it is a good thing to allow yourself now and then to abandon yourself to your friends or to others who wish you well.

There are other connections there too which you will discover beneath the hurry and forced relations of our everyday life. These connections have always been there, but, caught up in our wilful forging of our destiny, we have overlooked the simple, ordained sequence of the light and dark, or the orderly succession of the seasons.

Many grieving people find solace in returning to this order, which, after all, is more in tune with what they have now discovered about life: that death is as inevitable as winter; and that the rebirth after a death is as invincible as spring. Thus it is very common for a grieving person to take up gardening, for instance, because it is an activity that literally involves them in the cycles of death and rebirth, of planting and harvesting, of the old truths which make sense of dying and grieving in a way that our insistence on 'progress' through a 'happy' or 'successful' life does not.

reorientation: opening up

Grieving breaks us open. And although we may feel painfully vulnerable, it has the merit of breaking down the ordinary barriers we have learned to erect between ourselves and others.

Surprising discoveries may come with this new openness, if you are alert to them. The nature and kind of relationships you have now will probably be quite different than those you had before. The faithful friends are more valued. Having rejected the false comfort and the forced associations of earlier days, you are now better able to detect the true value of others and to appreciate them more keenly.

When you are grieving, you are changing, and coming to terms with change. So it follows that your relationships, too, will become different. Here are some examples:

angels and others

The period following a death – and this may extend to months or even years – is a very special time in someone's life. During this time, exceptional people may appear. They may not be people who figured in your previous life, or they may have figured only very marginally. They may find their way to you because they, too, have suffered a terrible grief. Or they may simply have been sent. If that sounds crazy, all I can say is: it is true. If you keep your eyes and heart open, you will find special people to help you during this special time. Some people describe them as 'angels' – which literally means a messenger.

When these people appear in your life, you will recognize them. Let them into your life and share your experience with them. They will help.

Of course the whole point of angels is that they fly away. You will probably find that, as you recover, these people perhaps return more to their own life, leaving you stronger and more able than you were to begin with.

It is important that you recognize that angels are transient – they are guides and momentary helpers. Do not seek to hold on to them or to burden the relationship beyond what it can bear.

Reassure yourself and them that they will always have a special place in your heart as one of those who have helped you find the way to your new life. Then let them go, blessing them as the messengers they have become.

second relationships

If you have lost your spouse, if you have lost your child or friend, there will be a lot of pressure to 'replace' him or her.

You are ready to begin a second relationship, to have another child, to look for another friend, when you realize that you can never replace the person you have lost.

Second relationships are different. They never replace the first; they occupy a different space. Moreover, it is important in a second relationship that the space left by the first always be acknowledged. That loss will always be a presence in your life now. But, rightly understood, that first relationship will be one that will augment, not threaten or impoverish your move into a new life.

Because you have loved once, you will be able to love again.

What grieving exposes are the false models by which we have been making our lives. In mourning, we come to understand how artificial happiness is and how hollow as a life-goal.

Goals themselves may become suspect, as we no longer understand life as a linear progression. If grieving in a 'happy' and 'successful' world is cruel, it does teach us to re-examine core values of our world, to reject those that emphasize permanence and self-sufficiency for values that allow us to be open to change and to find new connections with others.

A Woman Alone

When she cannot be sure
which of two lovers it was with whom she felt
this or that moment of pleasure, of something fiery
streaking from head to heels, the way the white
flame of a cascade streaks a mountainside
seen from a car across a valley, the car
changing gear, skirting a precipice,
climbing ...
When she can sit or walk for hours after a movie
talking earnestly and with bursts of laughter
with friends, without worrying
that it's late, dinner at midnight, her time
spent without counting the change...
When half her bed is covered with books
and no one is kept awake by the reading light
and she disconnects the phone, to sleep till noon ...
Then
selfpity dries up, a joy
untainted by guilt lifts her.
She has fears, but not about loneliness;
fears about how to deal with the aging
of her body – how to deal
with photographs and the mirror. She feels
so much younger and more beautiful
than she looks. At her happiest
– or even in the midst of
some less than joyful hour, sweating
patiently through a heatwave in the city
or hearing the sparrows at daybreak, dully gray,
toneless, the sound of fatigue –
a kind of sober euphoria makes her believe
in her future as an old woman, a wanderer,
seamed and brown,

little luxuries of the middle of life all gone,
watching cities and rivers, people and mountains,
without being watched; not grim nor sad,
an old winedrinking woman, who knows
the old roads, grass-grown, and laughs to herself...
She knows it can't be:
that's Mrs. Doasyouwouldbedoneby from

The Water Babies

no one can walk the world any more,
a world of fumes and decibels.
But she thinks maybe
she could get to be tough and wise, some way,
anyway. Now at least
she is past the time of mourning,
now she can say without shame or deceit,
O blessed Solitude.

Denise Levertov

nine: directions to another place

The first instinct after a bereavement is to freeze. To stay still, to keep everything as it was, is an instinctive fear reaction. If so much has changed so suddenly, one can reason that the sensible thing now is to try to limit change in hopes of limiting the damage inflicted by change.

However, even in practical things, everything starts moving very rapidly when someone dies. There are things that have to be arranged at short notice: a funeral, a burial, a reorganization of immediate priorities. After that, there is a lull. Take advantage of this, and once the practical necessities are looked after, try to proceed at your own pace. Many things can be left to be done in their own time, when you have the strength and energy.

As opposed to frenzied practical activity, or schedules for clearing out and reorganizing your life, what you should do now is seek some inner stillness. Try to make time to act from within – to visit places that were significant, to place flowers on the grave, or just to stare out the window.

Yet it is important to remember that staying still is impossible if you are to remain alive. To move is to live. To resist change is to die. But to continue living requires courage, and an ability to imagine a direction – so that, in some sense, you can direct change.

reorientation: a journey to another country

Grieving is often imagined as a journey.

The difficulty of the journey model is that it seems to presume some sort of progress. For, rather than progress, the bereaved person may often feel he is going backwards rapidly. He may cry uncontrollably. She may not be able to make decisions, or even to read.

What death feels like is chaos. You are not in control. Others will treat you like an invalid, or even a child. You yourself feel you can barely cope, and sometimes in fact you cannot cope at all. It feels like disintegration; it feels like hell. The last thing you need to be told now is that you are on a journey, for it feels as if all journeys have stopped and all the clocks have frozen; as if you have stepped out of time together with the one who died.

Yet, although the journey is not at times a useful model for immediate grief, over the length of years it is clear that a journey has been made.

The experience that seems to come closest to that of grieving is that of changing countries.

Emigration is a form of death. Everyone that has left their own country for an unknown place knows this implicitly, but perhaps the parallels have never been explicitly spelled out.

Here are the things that predictably will happen when you change countries:

- You are lost; you do not know your way around.
- You are emotionally disoriented.
- You are grieving for those you left behind.
- You are grieving for the place you left behind.
- You will be gradually stripped of a sense of self, as your origins, family, class, and acquired skills are unlikely to be recognized in the new venue.
- You will be stereotyped.
- You are unlikely to be recognized for who you are. In your own eyes, you may not even recognize yourself.
- You will probably find yourself confined to a ghetto of other émigrés, who may seek to initiate you into the new world you have entered. But, in doing so, they will also offer their own stereotypes of this new world. This ghetto may be an actual social circle or simply a state of mind.
- You will thrive insofar as you are able to reorient yourself, make new connections, resist stereotyping, and break out of the ghetto.
- As in a new country, you will have an exceptional chance to remake yourself and to find a new life.

The parallels to the experience of loss are obvious:

- You are lost, missing your usual orientation in the one you love.
- The loss may involve a loss of status, income, perhaps family connections, and even those of class.
- You may be sidelined, put mentally into the ghetto of the suffering.
- Stereotyped as a 'widow' or 'survivor', you may feel you are not recognized for who you are. You may not even feel you recognize yourself.
- You will suffer a profound sense of loss and nostalgia for the old life you have left behind.
- But, as in a new country, you now have an exceptional opportunity to remake yourself and to find a new life.

To use emigration as a metaphor for grieving is helpful in indicating both the degree of loss – and of hope.

What grieving accomplishes is to move you to a new place in your mind. You will never again have the unquestioning sense of belonging that you had in your previous life. That security is gone. Now you are in a different world, where people disappear, where there are no answers to the big questions, where there is pain and uncertainty. But death has moved us here, and the new place has the advantages of allowing us to remake our lives here under these newly-perceived conditions. In this new country we are 'lost,/Unhappy and at home'.

On a practical level, the emigration model is useful in indicating certain stages, and degrees, of pain, as well as the grounds of hope for a new life. In psychological terms, this model is also useful in indicating the usual time span for the period of adjustment. Most international organizations which co-opt personnel from foreign countries seek to repatriate them within two or three years. The reason for this is that it is generally accepted that after three years one has 'moved' psychologically into the new country and repatriation thus becomes more difficult if one stays any longer.

For the grieving, indicating some time span for the adjustment to loss is helpful – even if three years seems a very long time to someone in the first acute stages of loss.

For the grieving, too, this model is helpful in indicating that they will never fully 'belong' to the new territory to which they have moved. Like most emigrants, they will still mourn for the past and the old country from which they came; and like most emigrants, they will hold that place in their hearts even while they make their life anew among the opportunities of a new place. In that sense, one is never 'at home' again.

reorientation: travelling

Do not make the mistake of thinking that any of this will happen quickly. Most people think that they will be 'better' in one year, maybe a little longer. Then when they do not feel 'better' in a year, they sink into despair (and many grieving people may find the second year actually more difficult).

In real terms, the time span for entering this new life is much the same as becoming acculturated to a new country: about three to five years. During this time, you may feel not unlike a refugee: not at home and not recognized for who you are – and perhaps not even recognizable to yourself.

What the journey model tells us is what death underlines. We are all pilgrims. We are not at home in this world, but moving through it.

For this reason, at some time after the first chaotic period of grieving, and as part of your reorganizing of your life, it is helpful to travel: if only because travel becomes itself an image of our lives, which have been uprooted by death. An excursion elsewhere, with someone you care for, may allow you to find a neutral space in which to grieve and think about what comes next. It allows you to concentrate on yourself and your needs without the demands of a job or extended family and to move outside the normal expectations of society. It allows you to broaden your world, and to understand that your experience is not unique.

Finally, it allows you to come home, and, in doing so, to look at your life with new eyes: to see what needs to be done next, to have the strength to begin the necessary reorganization which will lead you to another life.

dead-end: shrinking your grief

This is the model most people have of grief: as some big, overwhelming thing that shrinks over time.

Imagine a large glass jar. You are given three rubber balls: one the size of the large jar; another medium-sized; another, a very small ball.

For your first act, you stuff the large ball into the large jar; it barely fits. Look at the result: one squashed ball in a jar. That is the way recent grief feels to most people. It fills everything. There is no margin for anything else. There is no room to manoeuvre, even to breathe. Grief has taken over all the available emotional space in your world. There is nothing left over.

Pull out the large ball (difficult). Put in the medium-sized ball. Look at the jar and ball now. If the ball represents grief, the grief appears to have shrunk. If the jar represents your life, we notice how much more room there is within it: the ball can move around; there is space for other thoughts, other feelings.

Take out this ball and put in the smallest ball. If the ball represents grief, we can now almost ignore it. At the very least, the grief is now manageable. It rolls around in the space. There is plenty of room for other thoughts, other feelings; and (who knows?) at this rate the ball might even shrink some more until it simply disappears.

This is a model for grief that is convenient for others, because it allows them to think that you will 'get better' as your grief 'shrinks'. But this is a very threatening model for the bereaved, because from the beginning they suspect that the grief – although in the long term it may not be as painful – will always be the same shape and size. Moreover, the bereaved do not wish to lose their grief: it is their last tie with the person they loved. To lose their grief, or to lessen it, again seems to diminish the extent of the loss they have suffered and the value of the person they have lost.

reorientation: growing your world

Take another model, more useful.

Imagine three glass jars: one small, one medium-sized, one large. Take only one ball, exactly the size of the smallest jar.

Place it first in the small jar. You can barely squeeze it in.

Then pull it out and place it in the second, bigger jar; there is more room.

Finally, drop the ball into the third and largest jar. There is lots of room now.

But the ball has not changed its shape or size. The grief is still the same shape and size.

It is the jar that has gotten bigger.

This model is a better one for picturing your task: it does not shrink or diminish your grief, or imply that it can be shrunk

or diminished. It defines the real work of grieving as making your world larger, so that the grief will be contained in an environment in which you can still move around and live and breathe, even though you still carry your grieving within you.

Children are said to survive grief more successfully than older people because their worlds are still growing. Older people sometimes respond to grief by trying to keep everything exactly the same. They do not wish to change anything. Is it not change, in the shape of death, that has already devastated them? Why should they then invite further change into their lives?

But one must understand: change is inevitable, just as death is, whether we wish it or not. It is important to try to embrace change, on the understanding that, with the death that has bereaved you, you are also entering a new life, a life which can be larger, richer, more challenging than the one you have left behind.

Your task as a bereaved person, your grief-work, is to enlarge your world. Imagine you are like a child, starting over again, but starting all over with the advantages of experience, an education, family and friends who support you. Then imagine the glass jar which is your world: how can you make it larger so that you can accommodate your grief but not be overwhelmed by it? There are some obvious ways: travel, for instance, can enlarge your world – also meeting new people, taking an extension course at a university, learning a new skill.

There are few opportunities in life for beginning over again; death, for all its pain, allows the bereaved a chance to remake their life. Take heart, and take your life into your own hands. After a death one has at least the advantage of having not much else to lose – or fear. Few things as bad can happen again.

time and death

When you look back on the days or hours before someone close to you died, that time takes on a preternatural significance. It seems as if every gesture, every word, every thought is enlarged. You scrutinize each minute of those last days to find clues to the meaning of their death. Sometimes this sense of enlarged, anticipatory significance happens even before the

The last Night that She lived
It was a Common Night
Except the Dying – this to Us
Made Nature different

We noticed smallest things –
Things overlooked before
By this great light upon our minds
Italicized – as 'twere.

As We went out and in
Between Her final Room
And Rooms where Those to be alive
Tomorrow, were, a Blame

That others could exist
While She must finish quite
A Jealousy for Her arose
So nearly infinite –

We waited while She passed –
It was a narrow time –
Too jostled were Our Souls to speak
At length the notice came.

She mentioned, and forgot –
Then lightly as a Reed
Bent to the Water, struggled scarce –
Consented, and was dead –

And We – We placed the Hair –
And drew the Head erect –
And then an awful leisure was
Belief to regulate –

Emily Dickinson

death, as if one somehow knew that this was going to happen.

After the death, it is as if you have stepped out of time. Events seem to occur in some parallel universe, as if time itself had been widened and stretched or you had broken a hole into the weave of our measured days and come into a place which exists outside them. The poet Wordsworth called these moments 'spots of time' – but really he meant 'spots of eternity'.

Grieving too is like this. Years after someone has died, we will find ourselves back with them in a certain moment, outside of any given time. Grieving itself opens this door for us, the door that allows us to move beyond the gates of perception into another world. Another name for it is the world of imagination, which moves beyond our ordinary notions of time but provides a new perspective on how we live within them.

creativity as a response to death

Death single-handedly initiates us into another world. For some, this world may be expressed in completely orthodox terms: death reveals to us the truth of an eternal life, outside of time. Death implies resurrection.

But for many who sorrow, this is too easy. Sometimes the Christian response feels as if it had become too abstract, as if it had left out the suffering.

For our experience begins in pain, a pain very close to fear, and a fear at times close to terror. We now know that death is a kind of violence. It has taken away someone we love. It has taken away the life we had with them. One day it will also take us.

How do we respond? We know we have a choice: to die with the one we loved. Or to create a new life.

This cannot be done merely by force of will, but by choosing to submit to the process of transformation. Whether we imagine this as the cycle of nature, by which winter moves inexorably, without any intervention from us, into summer; or whether we chose to adopt the Christian formula that death will bring new life – this is up to us. Each are different way of phrasing the promise of hope: that resurgence will come if we trust to the possibility of new life and are prepared to open ourselves to it.

In that trust are the grounds for remaking our own lives. We must do so if only because the life we had created has disappeared with the person who died. The expected future for our dead child; the plans we had made with our dead spouse; the past we had constructed with our siblings and parents – all these have vanished when they died. It is said that when your child dies, you have lost your future; and when your spouse or parents or a sibling dies, you have lost your past. What you recall of those futures and those pasts were the work of your imagination, as it elaborated real events or real potentialities. Now it is up to you to make another future – and construct another past – for yourself.

making a difference

Whatever happens from now on, you must resolve that life will be different, even if it remains superficially the same.

Tokens of difference in your private life should be markers of how your life has changed.

Making a difference can take a larger form. One mother who lost both her children started a movement for the first children's hospice in Ireland, so that other dying children would have a place where they could die with dignity and in the presence of their family.

Now is the chance to do that thing you always wanted to do. This is the time to take your courage into your own hands and determine that, because someone you loved died, it will change the way you – and others – now live.

imagining your story

All of us have stories, and in some sense we are the stories we tell about ourselves.

The death of a parent or a sibling or a spouse puts their stories under question. You may suddenly realize how little you knew about them, even if you have lived for years with them. In reviewing your relationship, you will probably come to know and to understand them better.

With the death of a baby or a child you have lost a story about your future. This is also true of the loss of a spouse, as you would have planned ahead, even if only on the scale of a few years.

One way of looking at death is that it has now given you the freedom to discover a new story. You may wish to become the custodian of your parents' history – or that of your spouse. Inevitably, too, you will find yourself making a story about what your child or brother or sister might have been doing, had they lived. For you, these may even live in a parallel imaginative universe, growing up, marrying, having children, growing old. Imagination has given you this grace, that they may exist in that way for you as long as you live.

But the most important thing is that death, any death, has given you the opportunity now to remake your own story.

You get to choose – from any life you can imagine for yourself.

Or you may choose not to take control of your story. But do not think that by *not* choosing, you will avoid pain or trouble. What will happen is that you will simply fall into the tired old script of the widow or widower or bereaved person, whose life goes the same old round until it simply grinds to a halt. That is another kind of death and is the price of not having the courage to envisage another future for yourself other than the dreary one that society has dictated for you.

The true work of grieving is that of imagining, and thus recreating, your life. So take up your pen, and list the things you want out of life now – despite your impulse to give yourself up to despair, exhaustion, and pain. You can remake your life once you can imagine it. And, along with remaking your life, you can imagine the new life that your beloved and dead other self has entered into: a life radiant, free, joyous, and full of peace.

finding equivalents

Emerging from this extraordinary experience, the grieving often seek to find some expression for it, as an objective equivalent. They seek something that will involve them again, but at a distance now, in the life-changing experience of encountering and enduring death.

For some, that equivalent may be the rituals of an established religion; they may go back to church and find comfort

Into the Hour

I have come into the hour of a white healing.
Grief's surgery is over and I wear
The scar of my remorse and my feeling.

I have come into a sudden sunlit hour
When ghosts are scared to corners. I have come
Into the time when grief begins to flower

Into a new love. It has filled my room
Long before I recognized it. Now
I speak its name. Grief finds its good way home.

The apple-blossom's handsome on the bough
And Paradise spreads round. I touch its grass.
I want to celebrate but don't know how.

I need not speak though everyone I pass
Stares at me kindly. I would put my hand
Into their hands. Now I have lost my loss

In some way I may later understand.
I hear the singing of the summer grass.
And love, I find, has no considered end,

Nor is subject to the wilderness
Which follows death. I am not a traitor to
A person or a memory. I trace

Behind that love another which is running
Around, ahead. I need not ask its meaning.

Elizabeth Jennings

there. For others, death may have initiated a search among other ancient wisdom for some response to the unanswered, the unanswerable questions.

Others may find that they now read or hear or see with a new acuity. The intense presences of art may now speak to them with voices they never heard before, or with visions only previously intuited. They may suddenly understand what Rilke means when he writes, 'For Beauty's nothing/but the beginning of Terror we're still just able to bear ...' or what Wallace Stevens is trying to say in the line: 'Death is the mother of Beauty'.

Death *is* the mother of beauty. The equivalents we find – never equivalent – are what we make of the paradox of human life: that human beings love, and love what vanishes. That is all that can be said; but the saying of it counts for something.

loving

Only people who are capable of loving strongly can also suffer great sorrow; but this same necessity of loving serves to counteract their grief and to heal them.

Because you loved once, you are able to love again. Because you once loved someone, they will remain with you always. Your grieving is a way of finding ways in which you will recover them: by making a new life in which they still have a central place; in acknowledging their presence in the way you choose to remake your life. Your grieving will make a difference: in the way you live now; in the person you are to become.

Love is not circumscribed. It is not limited. It will not run out. Loving someone who is now dead changes the mode of loving, but also extends its reach. In grieving, you have been initiated into a world where you now will see things differently. You will now have the ability to see that others, too, are suffering. You now have the ability to console, because you understand and share their pain. You now belong to a world that is larger, more comprehensive. You have become enriched, not impoverished by your pain. And you have become at last someone in your own right. Now you may ask, with the poet Rilke,

Is it not time that, in loving,/we freed ourselves
from the loved one,
and, quivering, endured:/as the arrow endures the
string, to become,
in the gathering out-leap,/something more than
itself?

Having worked hard to complete our grieving, it is time to free
ourselves, and to become, in one great gathering leap, someone
more than our mere sorrowing selves.

What Are Years?

What is our innocence,
what is our guilt? All are
        naked, none is safe. And whence
is courage: the unanswered question,
the resolute doubt, –
dumbly calling, deafly listening – that
in misfortune, even death,
        encourages others
        and in its defeat, stirs

        the soul to be strong? He
sees deep and is glad, who
        accedes to mortality
and in his imprisonment rises
upon himself as
the sea in a chasm, struggling to be
free and unable to be,
        in its surrendering
        finds its continuing.

        So he who strongly feels,
behaves. The very bird,
        grown taller as he sings, steels
his form straight up. Though he is captive,
his mighty singing
says, satisfaction is a lowly
thing, how pure a thing is joy.
        This is mortality,
        this is eternity.

Marianne Moore

ten: guidelines for spirit guardians

If you are close to someone who is bereaved, you have a special role to play. It is not perhaps a part you would have chosen, but how you play it out will make a significant difference to the way in which the bereaved will eventually come to terms with their grieving. And, along the way, you too may come to understand something about the nature of the terms involved, whether they are about loss or death or simply about our relation to the world and to each other.

It is a rare chance to understand what love really means.

How well you can care for your bereaved friend or family depends too on your orientation to grief. Here are a few suggestions about what is helpful and what is not.

do not try to fix the problem

The one big thing you have to remember is that grief is not a problem to be fixed. Nor is the person grieving a problem to be fixed.

Grieving is the response to loss, which is inevitable. Judging the extent or worth of the loss is not your role.

You are there to feel the loss with those who grieve, and to value it at their value, and, in sharing it, to suffer with them. That is what compassion means.

What the grieving encounter are not problems. They are face to face with fundamental and insoluble difficulties – those that define the very core and meaning of our existence. Do not demean them by underestimating either their grieving or the hard questions it raises. In encountering loss they are learning what it is to live; for no one can live fully until they have understood that life is tragedy.

And grieving is the process by which one learns that lesson.

what is helpful

Those who are close to the bereaved, please note: grief is a profound experience. It is also a valuable one. Grief immediately detects what is false, what is shabby, what is only half-true.

Good intentions on your part are not enough. If you wish to help the grieving, you must do so honestly. Inevitably you will also feel pain. If you cannot bear the pain or seek to deflect it in ways that are less than authentic, you will only add to it – and it is best in such circumstances that you do something from a distance, such as writing a letter, sending flowers, or making some gift in the dead person's name.

be exquisitely tender

Try to imagine the grieving person as someone in terrible physical pain, and that might give you some idea of how best to give comfort. Whole-hearted attention, a few quiet words, something good to eat: these are more effective in helping your grieving friend through their day than anything more direct or demonstrative.

be genuinely available

Grieving is unpredictable. At the oddest times, a grieving person may feel overwhelmed. Often these times are when others will be busy, or asleep, or away (as on holidays), or not normally available (as on Saturday nights). Obviously Christmas and the New Year are going to be difficult times.

If you really want to help someone who is grieving, and you feel you can do it in good grace, it is wonderful if you can say: 'Listen, I know you don't know when you will need this: but if you have a really bad moment, I hope you will phone me, even if it's suppertime or the middle of the night.'

Never offer to be available if you do not feel that you can be. And if someone does actually phone, and it's at a bad time, arrange to ring them back as soon as possible.

listen *(as if your life depended on it – their life may)*

The grieving cannot be comforted. The grief cannot be fixed. Do not try to comfort. Do not try to fix the grieving person. To honour the pain of the grieving, the most important thing is to listen; listen quietly, without comment; listen with your heart. It will be painful. That is why people try to 'fix' grief; that is why people try to offer comfort. They do not want the pain to spread. But the best way to help someone to bear pain, is in one sense to let it spread. If you have the resources, see if you can simply absorb the pain. That way it is not intensified; it is accommodated, it is shared, it is understood.

do something rather than say something

Words are treacherous at this time and may do harm. A grieving person is very vulnerable; it is as if they have no defences, and anything you say will be imprinted on their heart forever. So be very careful what you say. Rather than say something, sometimes it is best simply to do something that shows how you feel. Prepare a special dish and leave it with your bereaved friend. Ask your friend out for a walk, and do not talk about the loss unless it is clear that that is what is wished for. Invite your friend out for a movie or a play: but be careful – painful or violent episodes or story-lines that are too close to what is happening in their own lives may make the outing a disaster.

be honest

Do not make gestures you do not mean to carry through, such as inviting the bereaved to dinner or promising to phone and then forgetting all about it or postponing the moment indefinitely. Note: if you do not honour these promises, you have only added to the pain. Do not say more than you mean. Do not promise more than you can do. But tell the grieving person what you can do – say, take them out to lunch on a certain day – and then do it.

acknowledge the pain

Accept the pain (do not deny it).
Do not try to fix the grief (it can't be fixed).
And don't try to fix the bereaved (there is nothing to fix).

exemplar: a conversation

My mother is beside herself with grief. She will literally die of it if it continues at this intensity. We have all done what we can. But she simply cannot face being alone after almost forty years of marriage. Yet she doesn't want to continue living with us, as she has done since the day of the funeral.

What are you doing about it?

We each phone her every day. My brother visits her every morning. She comes to us every week for dinner. But she still insists she is abandoned.

She says that?

Yes, she says she feels abandoned. But this is ridiculous. We are going nuts trying to make sure she knows we are around.

But she says she feels abandoned.

Yes, I don't know what we are going to do about it. She is killing herself with this grief.

Why do you think you have to do anything more than you have done?

Well, she still feels abandoned.

Well, that's the way you feel when someone you love dies. You feel you've been dumped, rejected, left to fend for yourself. Of course you feel abandoned.

But we want her to stop feeling this way. She is not abandoned by us.

But she has been abandoned by her husband. That's the way she feels. It isn't going to go away. Why are you trying to fix this? What about trying *not* to fix it? What about just sitting down and letting her talk about it? What about just saying: You are having a terrible time. You must feel very alone. And then just staying with her in that terrible lonely place for a while, so that she knows she is not alone in this pain?

what is not helpful

clichés/pious platitudes
Watch what you say. Do not offer cheap or threadbare phrases to those who are in profound suffering. They may not forgive you – nor should they.

Better to abide with the grieving in silence, seeking to enter and be with them in their pain, than to degrade it with platitudes. The wounded heart is easily bruised; honour it with words spoken thoughtfully or not at all.

avoiding the bereaved
Yes: they do notice that you have crossed the road pretending not to see them – and it adds to their pain.
Yes: they do notice you do not telephone them as often as you used to do – and it adds to their pain.
Yes: they did notice that they were not invited to the party or that wedding – and it added to their pain.

imposing your own agenda/schedule on their grieving
There is no 'right' way to grieve and no 'accepted' schedule for grieving. Attend to the way the grieving choose to grieve, without imposing your own expectations on them.

A note of caution: do not tell a grieving person about your experiences of grief – they can barely cope with their own pain, and certainly not with yours. If you have had a comparable experience, the best you can do for those who are grieving is to join them in silent companionship, one which acknowledges, by that very act, their pain. Avoid such phrases as 'I know how you feel'. Everyone grieves differently and for different losses; do not seek to take that away by some easy assumption that you can understand what they are going through. You can't; you can only accompany them to the place where they are and be with them there.

dismissing the importance of grieving
The grieving stand at the centre of an experience so intense, it can (and sometimes does) kill them. Or it can release them back

into a life that is larger and richer than the one they had before.

Rather, reassure them that you understand the crucial nature of this experience, that you understand they are making their passage back to that new life. If you can, seek to accompany them on that journey.

how to become a spirit guardian

The grieving live in pain that is like a wound; they cannot be protected from that pain, but need someone to help them through it.

To help the grieving, you must understand that what must be protected is their spirit. For all those difficult transitional moments, they need someone who understands how fragile and bruised they feel. They need someone to keep them from needlessly becoming exposed to further pain.

Such moments might be:

- when they must report in to identify a body;
- when they go in to say goodbye to the dead person;
- when they return after the funeral;
- when they must attend an inquest;
- when they first return to work after a bereavement;
- when they first return to an empty house or apartment after travelling away;
- when you know they will be alone and lonely: during holidays, during a long weekend, over their own birthday;
- when they face into the anniversaries: the first week, the first month, the first years of the death – when they face into those hidden anniversaries, such as that of the day of their marriage.

There are any number of moments when those who are grieving need not a bodyguard, but a spirit-guard, who will help them across the thresholds of their new world. On their first day back from work, if you are a colleague, meet them at the office door, bring them into the office and get them coffee. Stay with them for a while, or return for lunch. Or, after their first trip away, meet your grieving friend at the airport and drive them home. Walk into the empty house with them and stay for a cup of tea, then leave. Perhaps phone later.

Use your imagination. Think ahead to when the worst moments might occur in the next days or weeks or even months. Then offer to meet and accompany your friend wherever they need to go. You are not required to do more than to understand they live with a pain that is like a wound, and that they live with the fear that anything less than the most exquisite tenderness will cause them irreparable harm.

Remember: You are here to guard their spirit.

reminder to friends

Grieving is not a problem to be fixed. Nor is the grieving person a problem to be fixed.

There is no short cut or magic pill or formula that will cure grief. The pain is inevitable and unavoidable.

The aim of grieving is not recovery, because, in some radical sense, one never recovers.

The aim of grieving is acceptance: acceptance of the loss of someone loved; acceptance of pain; recognition of the inevitability of death.

With such acceptance comes a reconciliation to the suffering that is at the centre of human existence – and with it, peace.

Friends: You have much to learn from the grieving.
Listen.
Accompany.
Attend.

Acknowledgements

John Cornford, 'Huesca', from 'Full Moon at Tierz: Before the Storming of Huesca', JOHN CORNFORD: COLLECTED WRITINGS, edited by Jonathan Galassi (Carcanet Press Limited, 1986).

Gérard de Nerval, 'The Grandmother', trans. Barbara Howes, from TRANSLATIONS BY AMERICAN POETS, ed. Jean Garigue (Ohio University Press, 1970).

Emily Dickinson, F339 'I like a look of agony'; F372 'After great pain, a formal feeling comes'; F 591 'I heard a fly buzz when I died'; F1100 'The last night that she lived'. Reprinted by permission of the publishers and the Trustees of Amherst College from THE POEMS OF EMILY DICKINSON, Ralph W. Franklin, ed., Cambridge, Mass.: The Belknap Press of Harvard University Press, Copyright © 1998 by the President and Fellows of Harvard College. Copyright © 1951, 1955, 1979, 1983 by the President and Fellows of Harvard College.

Tess Gallagher, 'Yes', MY BLACK HORSE: NEW & SELECTED POEMS (Bloodaxe Books, 1995), reprinted by permission of International Creative Management, Inc. Copyright © 1995 by Tess Gallagher.

Tony Harrison, 'Long Distance 11', from SELECTED POEMS (Penguin, 1987).

Elizabeth Jennings, 'Into the Hour', from NEW COLLECTED POEMS, edited by Michael Schmidt (Carcanet Press Limited, 1986).

Denise Levertov, 'A Woman Alone', from LIFE IN THE FOREST, copyright © by Denise Levertov. Reprinted by permission of New Directions Publishing Corporation and also by permission of Pollinger Limited and the proprietor.

Marianne Moore, 'What Are Years?' Reprinted with the permission of Scribner, an imprint of Simon & Schuster Adult Publishing Group and Faber and Faber Ltd., from THE COLLECTED POEMS by Marianne Moore. Copyright © 1941 by Marianne Moore; copyright renewed ©1969 by Marianne Moore.

Pablo Neruda, 'Amor', poem published in the magazine CLARIDAD © Fundación Pablo Neruda, 1922; translated as 'Love', by Margaret Sayers Peden, from PASSIONS AND IMPRESSIONS, ed. Matilde Neruda and Miguel Otero Silva (Farrar, Straus, Giroux, 1983), p. 4.

Linda Pastan, 'The Five Stages of Grief', from THE FIVE STAGES OF GRIEF, copyright ©1978 by Linda Pastan. Used by permission of W.W. Norton & Company, Inc.

Carole Satyamurti, 'Changing the Subject (6. How Are You?)', from STITCHING IN THE DARK: NEW & SELECTED POEMS (Bloodaxe Books, 2005).

Dylan Thomas, 'Do Not Go Gentle into that Good Night', from COLLECTED POEMS (Dent) and THE POEMS OF DYLAN THOMAS copyright © 1952 by Dylan Thomas. Reprinted by permission of New Directions Publishing Corporation.

Andrew Young, 'Passing the Graveyard', from SELECTED POEMS, edited by Edward Lowbury and Alison Young (Carcanet Press Limited, 1998).

Illustrations on pp. 114 and 115 by Sarah John.

notes

p. 13 St Bernard, 'To the Stabbed Side of Jesus', trans. by John Gray, *Spiritual Poems* (1896), reprinted in *The Poems of John Gray*, ed. Ian Fletcher, 1880–1920 British Author Series No. 1 (Greensboro, North Carolina: ELT Press, 1988), pp. 110–11.

p. 13 'Through the little hole of his wound …' James Hillman, referring to Hans Castorp in *The Magic Mountain*, and the spot of tuberculosis which has appeared on Castorp's lung, as quoted by Robert Bly in *Iron John: A Book about Men* (New York: Addison-Wesley Publishing Company, Inc., 1990), p. 209.

p. 16 'In the seventeenth century …' Such works as Jeremy Taylor's *The Rule and Exercises of Holy Dying* (1651) taught readers how to prepare for their own deaths.

p. 18 'Kisa Gotami's first baby …' from *The Tibetan Book of the Dead*, ed. W.Y. Evans-Wentz (Oxford University Press, 1968).

pp. 23–4 'The Terrors of Secrets' (interview with actress Charlotte Rampling), *The Irish Times*, Monday 1 September 2003, p. 12.

p. 27 'be patient toward all that is unsolved …' Ranier Maria Rilke, *Letters to a Young Poet*, trans. by Herter Norton (New York: W. W. Norton, 1962).

p. 29 'The writer Margaret Drabble…' Recounted in a review of Lavinia Greacan's *J. G. Farrell: The Making of a Writer* (London: Bloomsbury, 1999) by Gerald Dawe for *The Sunday Tribune*, 8 August 1999, p. 8.

p. 37 'To lose one parent…' Lady Bracknell in Act I of Oscar Wilde's *The Importance of Being Earnest*.

p. 46 Chippawa woman; quoted in Robert Bly, *Iron John*, p. 224.

p. 57 'mass drowning tragedy …' These statistics were taken from the story 'Zeebrugge disaster "made lives of survivors better"', in *The Sunday Times*, 16 March 2003, p. 14.

p. 80 The Grief Recovery website is www.Grief-Recovery.com. *The Grief Recovery Handbook* by John W. James and Russell Friedman is published by HarperPerennial (New York, 1998) in association with the Grief Recovery Institute, which runs programs in both the United States and Canada.

p. 83 'wee … cow'rin', tim'rous beastie …' Robert Burns, 'To a Mouse'.

pp. 93–4 'Then I read …' This is part of the story of Anna's house, which is given in Gail Sheehy, *Middletown, America: One Town's Passage from Trauma to Hope* (New York: Random House, 2003), p. 370.

p. 97 'A drunken man who falls out of a cart ...' Taken from the *Teachings and Sayings of Chuang Tzu* [Zhuangzi], Section 19 (Mineola, New York: Dover Publications, 2001).

p. 98 Julian of Norwich (c.1342–1416), *Revelations of Divine Love*, The Thirteenth Revelation, Chapter 27.

pp. 102–103 'But perhaps the formulation ...' These two paragraphs are a close paraphrase of Judith Butler's meditation on mourning in *Precarious Life: The Powers of Mourning and Violence* (London: Verso, 2004), p. 21.

p. 112 'lost,/ Unhappy and at home.' Seamus Heaney, 'The Tollund Man', *New Selected Poems* (London: Faber and Faber, 1990), p. 32.

pp. 114–15 Balls and Jars. This is a demonstration model of the grieving process given in lectures to bereaved children by Barbara Monroe, Director, St Christopher's Hospice in London. I first heard it as a lecture titled 'Death, Loss, and the Adolescent' on 25 September 1997 as part of a HEBER conference held at University College, Dublin. It is given here by her kind permission.

p. 118 'spots of time' Wordsworth used the phrase in *The Prelude*, Book 12, lines 208–18.

p. 122 'For Beauty's nothing/but ...' Rainer Maria Rilke, 'The First Elegy', *Duino Elegies*, trans. by J. B. Leishman and Stephen Spender (New York: W. W. Norton and Company, 1939), p. 21.

p. 122 'Death is the mother of beauty ...' Wallace Stevens, 'Sunday Morning', *The Collected Poems of Wallace Stevens* (London: Faber and Faber, 1966), p. 69.

pp. 122–3 'Is it not time that ...' Rilke, 'The First Elegy', *Duino Elegies*, p. 23.